The
Natural
Childbirth
Book

The Natural Childbirth Book

Joyce Milburn & Lynnette Smith

BETHANY HOUSE PUBLISHERS
Minneapolis, Minnesota 55438
A Division of Bethany Fellowship, Inc.

All Scripture quotations are taken from the King James Version of the Bible unless otherwise noted.

Copyright © 1981
Joyce Milburn and Lynnette Smith
All rights reserved

Published by Bethany Fellowship, Inc.
6820 Auto Club Road, Minneapolis, Minnesota 55438

Printed in the United States of America

Library of Congress Cataloging in Publication Data

Milburn, Joyce, 1953-
    The natural childbirth book.

    Bibliography: p.
    1. Natural childbirth.   2. Infants—Care and hygiene.
I. Smith, Lynnette, 1951-   II. Title.
RG661.M54   618.4'5   81-4647
ISBN 0-87123-399-1 (pbk.)   AACR2

Dedication

To our own parents,
who first taught us of families and love;

And to our husbands and children,
who are still teaching us.

About the Authors

Joyce Milburn and Lynnette Smith are Lamaze instructors in a group called Genesia Childbirth Educators in Anaheim, California. Their goal is to promote better family beginnings among both Christian and non-Christian parents and they offer complete preparation for couples anticipating their child's birth.

The Milburn family

The Smith family

Foreword

My husband would choke if he knew what I am about to say—but let me say it anyway. This book makes me (almost) want to have another baby! As I read it, I relived the births of our four children, and marveled at the recent medical alternatives that now enrich the childbirth experience. The childbirths I knew had climaxed with seemingly impersonal procedures. I had carried those children through nine months of anticipation and intimacy, yet at the times of their deliveries, I was made to feel like an unessential hindrance. At a certain point, I was put to sleep and later awakened after the glorious climax was completed. The doctor and the baby seemed to be the stars, while I was just a spectator.

My poor husband was purposely excluded from the whole experience. I remember at the birth of one of our children, Tim stayed with me during labor as long as the nurse on duty would allow him. Every time she came in to check me, she treated him as if he were an intruder. She probably thought of him as a giant germ, eager to infect the hospital. She was an older nurse, and had been taught that the father was not too useful at the time of birth. My husband, not easily pushed around, asked the nurse if he could go into the delivery room with me—after all, this was our third child. She quickly retorted that the staff had no time to revive fainting fathers in the delivery room, so he was sentenced to the fathers' waiting room.

What a refreshing change has entered the world of childbirth! Today, fathers are prepared right along with mothers to participate in the birth of their offspring. Why should the father be deprived of sharing this exhilarating moment with the mother? Together they should be able to view the grand entrance, the first breath, of their child who has been fashioned and designed by Almighty God. It can even be a spiritual experience as they receive this gift from God's own hand—"Lo, children are an heritage of the Lord" (Ps. 127:3).

The pages that follow contain very helpful, practical suggestions for prospective parents as they prepare for the birth of their child. I salute the mothers and fathers who want children enough to plan and prepare to be good and effective parents. Proper parenting is a rewarding and satisfying accomplishment. I heartily recommend it!

Beverly LaHaye
El Cajon, CA

Contents

Introduction

You are about to become parents. Congratulations! In the coming months and years, expect to meet many exciting challenges and to undergo many changes. This baby will have a profound effect on your lives . . . and probably the lives of many others.

Parenthood is an awesome responsibility which often fills people with questions. In the face of such uncertainties, it is nice to know that one thing will *never* change: *God has a plan—a special design—for every single human being.*

Do you wonder what God's plan is for *you*? Do you wonder how this baby will affect your life? Your mate's? Your marriage? Do you wonder what giving birth feels like? Do you worry about how you will feed your baby, or how you'll learn to love him? Do you doubt your ability to be a good parent?

Our goal is to help you prepare for that exciting day when your baby is born. We do this by stressing Lamaze techniques of prepared childbirth. However, this alone cannot prepare you for everything you may experience during your labor and postpartum period. For this reason, you should also learn about the process of labor and delivery, possible variations of labor, hospital procedures, coaching techniques, induced labors, fetal monitors, forceps, medication, caesarean delivery, recovery and postpartum care, newborn evaluation and care, circumcision, jaundice, breastfeeding, and much more.

Another very important aspect of preparation is that of father participation. The role of the father-coach is important to the success of the birth experience. Studies have confirmed that the mere presence of the baby's father causes the mother to experience significantly less discomfort. However, we want fathers to do more than just lend their presence to the situation. They should take an active role in the prenatal preparation, labor, and delivery, and also in the postpartum period.

Mutual involvement of the baby's mother and father will undergird and strengthen their relationship as a family. They will be bonded together, and to the baby, more closely than they would have ever thought possible. The baby will also have the currently rare privilege of being bonded with *both* parents from the moment of birth.

The classes can do much for you, but the outcome of your labor (your degree of success) is up to you. It is up to you to nourish the mother-coach relationship. It is up to you to practice faithfully the breathing and relaxation exercises. It is up to you to insure that your nutrition is adequate. It is up to you to maintain a good, healthy mental and emotional outlook about the forthcoming event. Preparation for birth is not easy, but the rewards of that preparation are well worth the trouble.

We believe that this book will give scriptural answers to some of the questions you have as prospective and new parents. But don't allow it to replace a good childbirth preparation course, conducted by a qualified instructor. Our intention is to supplement and enhance the training you receive and to add a spiritual dimension to your training.

We encourage you to seek answers for yourself from God's Word and from other sources as well. In so doing, you will gain the confidence necessary to approach pregnancy, birth, and child-rearing in a positive and enjoyable manner. We want your "family beginning" to be a blessed, satisfying experience.

Joyce Milburn and Lynnette Smith

NOTE: For simplicity, all references to babies and children are in the male gender.

PART I

THE BIRTH OF A FAMILY

The greatest forces in the world are not the earthquakes and the thunderbolts. The greatest forces in the world are babies.
—E. T. Sullivan

CHAPTER 1

Our Circle of Love

*Therefore shall a man leave his father and his mother, and
shall cleave unto his wife: and they shall be one flesh.* (Gen. 2:24)

Circles of love, circles of love;
Sweet little baby, sent from above;
Circles of love, circles of love;
God gave you to us to cherish and love.
—Ellen Roweton[1]

When a man and a woman become husband and wife, they
set up a home of love and call themselves a "couple." On the day
that they see the evidence of their love emerge in the form of a
newborn infant, they cannot help but be deliriously happy.

Another birth also takes place that day—the birth of a FAMI-
LY. Suddenly life becomes infinitely more rewarding and meaningful. It also becomes more complex, as the parents focus their
attention on meeting the needs of this tiny person who, by his appearance on the scene, has already enlarged their circle of love.

Many changes occur in every family with the addition of each
new member—whether it is the first child or the tenth. Yet God,
in His loving wisdom, gives nine months to prepare for parenthood, and many family changes actually begin to take place during the nine months of pregnancy. If you are expecting a child,
you have probably already noticed subtle differences in your own
attitudes toward, and in your relationship with, those with whom
you live. In this chapter we will explore some of the physical and
emotional changes both parents may experience during pregnancy, and ways they can use the time of waiting to prepare for
the greater changes to come.

The First Three Months

Before I formed thee in the belly I knew thee; and before thou camest forth out of the womb I sanctified thee. (Jer. 1:5)

The first trimester (three-month period) of pregnancy is a time of great adjustment. The change from a nonpregnant state to one of pregnancy is quite a transformation! Suddenly there is another life flourishing within the woman's own body.

What began with the fusion of two cells, the sperm and the egg, is a genuine little person, even during the first three months. It is amazing how quickly the embryo acquires all the body parts necessary to be termed a "fetus." Only three weeks after conception, a tiny heart is beating regularly. His digestive system is forming, along with the respiratory system and reproductive organs. Even glands, kidneys, a liver, and the bladder become well formed in that short span of time.

The child's arms and legs are growing and fingers and toes gain definition—all in the first three weeks! By the time the mother-to-be is three months' pregnant, the child will have the beginnings of fingernails and a completely formed face. Physically he may already look much as he will at birth. Yet he is only three inches long and weighs just an ounce.

While the baby is developing at this tremendous rate, the mother is also undergoing many physical changes. She may experience tenderness and fullness in her breasts, frequent urination, excessive fatigue, lack of appetite, or nausea and vomiting. She should rest as much as possible, even if it means cutting back on her working hours or social life for a while. New strength and vitality will soon be coming.

Although the baby is still very tiny, he is growing rapidly and needs many nutrients. Thus, it is important for the mother to eat properly, even if she feels nauseated. Most women find that if they eat snacks high in protein every hour, or whenever they feel a new wave of nausea, the feeling of sickness is reduced greatly.

Many expectant mothers do not experience any of these symptoms. They know they are pregnant simply because they feel "different." This "different" feeling may be due to the tremendous hormonal changes that are taking place in the mother's body, and are linked to the emotional upheavals characteristic to early pregnancy. Though she is generally excited over her newfound secret, mood swings and anxiety are very common. The husband often feels responsible for his wife's moodiness, and is laden with guilt whenever she begins to cry. One husband we know was scared to come home from work, not knowing if he would be greeted with tears or hysterical laughter! But there is really no need to worry. As her pregnancy progresses, the woman's emotions become more stable and predictable. But be prepared for anything; even in the most well-calculated pregnancies there can be emotional "surprises."

This emotional stress that newly expectant parents may feel can be intensified by worries about the future. Can we afford a baby? How will I finish college? Will we be able to live on one paycheck? Are we mature enough to be parents? It helps to talk over these matters with each other, but don't allow them to become fuel for worry or arguments. *Things will work out!* If the husband demonstrates extra patience and tenderness, the wife will respond with appreciation. He should also keep his expectations simple, for the time being, and trust in God to meet his needs.

Remember, the person who always understands and is able to lift you up *and* handle your problems is the Lord. Tell Him your concerns and worries, and then leave them with Him. "Casting all your care upon him, for he careth for you" (1 Pet. 5:7).

WORKING TOGETHER

Throughout this book you will find sections like this one. They are designed to bring husband and wife closer together, physically, emotionally, mentally, and spiritually. At appropriate intervals throughout your pregnancy, come together at a quiet time and place. Sit close to one another, touching. Before you begin, pray together, asking the Lord to help you understand each other's viewpoint. *Both* should answer each of the following questions, unless otherwise indicated.

The First Trimester

1. What are some of the emotions you have been experiencing during these early months?

2. How has your partner expressed understanding of these emotions?

3. What do you hope this baby's birth will be like?

4. What kind of effort are you making to find a doctor and hospital that will help you achieve this?

5. Whom do you consider to be good fathers or mothers? Why?

The Middle Months

And thou shalt have joy and gladness. (Luke 1:14)

The second trimester is a time of joy. Before this time the mother had jumbled emotions. She felt pregnant but no one else could tell. Now her expanding waistline makes her condition obvious to everyone. She acquires a beautiful radiance and sense of well-being.

This glow can partially be attributed to the joy of first feeling her baby's movements. This is traditionally called "quickening," which means "to come to life." Although he has been moving for some time already, these first movements felt by the mother make the baby seem more alive to her. For a woman, there is nothing that can compare to actually *feeling* her baby *living* inside of her! Before long, the father will also be able to feel this living child if the mother directs his hand to the right places. This seems to be a great landmark for almost every dad, and as he observes his wife's enlarging abdomen, he may be overcome with awe at the life that is blooming within her.

Your baby is blooming indeed! During the fourth month alone he doubles in length (to 6 or 7 inches), and his weight quadruples to four ounces. By the end of the sixth month he will weigh about 1½ pounds. His skin is red and wrinkly, like a baggy suit of clothes, and he is covered with a white creamy substance called vernix caseosa which protects and waterproofs his skin. Your baby is a whole little person now, but he is still very dependent upon his mother. He must grow, gain weight and mature, so that he can function on his own when he enters our world.

Before your child is born, take an objective look at the world he will be entering. In many ways your child is like a tender young plant. Any gardener can tell you that rich, fertile soil is needed to produce strong, healthy foliage. Likewise, your child must be nurtured in a warm and loving family to develop a well-balanced personality.

From a very early age your child will observe the type of relationship you have with your mate and be affected by it. Will he sense tension or peace? Will he see cold indifference or playful affection? Will he hear self-serving arguments or considerate, understanding discussions?

Perhaps you have serious problems in your marriage. There may have been several years of difficulty, mistrust, or bitterness which have built a high wall between the two of you. You may feel that it is impossible for anything good to come of your union. But be assured that God brought the two of you together in the first place. And He has a divine plan for both of you—as a couple. "With God *all things* are possible" (Matt. 19:26).

Ed Wheat, a Christian medical doctor devoted to helping couples with marital difficulties, teaches that marriage consists of *giving*—not 50-50 but 100% of yourself in an endeavor to please your mate. He says that if even just one partner in the marriage applies the principles of *giving* in love, the marriage can't help but improve. And if both partners apply it, their marriage will be a "little bit of heaven on earth."[2] This principle is consistent with Jesus' promise, "Give and it shall be given unto you; good measure pressed down, and shaken together, and running over. . . " (Luke 6:38).

We suggest that, if your marriage "soil" is unhealthy, you seek the guidance you need before you face the added stress of a new baby. Your pastor may be able to help you, or you may find that books or tapes by recognized Christian professionals will provide just the answer you are seeking.

The only love your child will learn is that which he sees and experiences firsthand in his own home. The only course on marriage he may ever take is the one you conduct daily in your own relationship. You owe it to your child to prepare for him a rich soil—a home filled with love and joy that will give him a taste of heaven on earth.

WORKING TOGETHER

The Second Trimester

1. Name five ways in which your partner has demonstrated love and concern for you during this pregnancy.

2. Write down ten things you appreciate about your partner and share these with him/her.

3. What qualities should a good mother have?

4. What qualities should a good father have?

5. Do you have any fears related to your baby's birth which you have not discussed together?

6. Have you turned all your worries over to the Lord?

Commit thy way unto the Lord; trust also in him; and he shall bring it to pass. (Ps. 37:5)

The Final Stretch

To every thing there is a season, and a time to every purpose under the heaven. . . . A time to be born, and a time to die; a time to plant, and a time to pluck up that which is planted; he hath made everything beautiful in its time. (Eccles. 3:1, 2, 11)

As the day of the baby's birth approaches, most parents are positive and enthusiastic. There is a heightened sense of anticipation, like that of a child looking forward to Christmas. Their wait is nearly over!

During the last three months an expectant mother's countenance is often peaceful—she has a feeling of "oneness with nature." She likes to dream of what her baby will be like.

For you, this is becoming easier every day: his increasing size and his frequent kicks, bumps, turns, wiggles, and even hiccups seem calculated to make every organ of your body aware of his presence. You may have greater difficulty getting comfortable and staying that way, but this is frequently overshadowed by the thrill of the approaching "birth-day." Shortness of breath, indigestion, pelvic pressure, and backaches seem a small price to pay for the love and happiness you will soon be sharing with this little person.

Most discomforts of late pregnancy are due simply to the fact that your baby is daily becoming larger and taking up more space inside you. In these three months he will progress from 1½ pounds to his final birth weight of 6-9 pounds. No wonder you are still gaining weight!

It is important to keep on eating, even though you have already surpassed the weight gain you intended, and your stomach is being crowded by Baby. Besides adding several pounds and inches, he is busy building and adding brain cells. For this reason, foods high in protein are especially important now. They will allow the greatest brain development at this crucial time.

Mother and Baby are not the only ones who experience changes during the last trimester; Father often undergoes a few himself. Up to this point, he enjoyed feeling and watching the baby's movements veiled by his wife's abdomen. He was content to share the delight she expressed about what was happening to her.

But as the time of birth draws near, he may develop a strong desire to know the child as intimately as she does. He is finally able to perceive her pregnancy in greater depth and to realize that a *baby* is joining them. He will often take a greater interest than before in other people's babies and in preparing for his own special newcomer.

This deeper realization of the impending birth makes enrollment at Lamaze classes during these last months especially important. As you both learn the information and exercises necessary to make your child's birth memorable, the father will begin to see the significance of his presence and assistance. He will discover ways to become more involved with his wife and baby. He will feel important—and he *should*!

We recommend Lamaze preparation because, of all the methods presently being taught, it appears to have a far higher proportion of students satisfied and thrilled with its results. Sign up for these classes well in advance, as they often fill up quickly. Don't hesitate to shop around, however, before committing yourselves. You want the very best!

Lamaze classes will help you develop a level of confidence that cannot be equalled by any amount of home study. It is important to have the weekly contact with a qualified instructor who can answer your questions, correct your errors, and reinforce your enthusiasm. Please do not attempt to teach yourselves childbirth techniques, or expect to learn them from a friend, or study hastily in the hospital labor room. A good series of classes will benefit both of you and give you the knowledge and self-assurance necessary for the best birth possible.

NATURAL CHILDBIRTH PRAISED*

by Jon Van

Women trained in the Lamaze method of natural childbirth have fewer problems delivering babies, according to a study at Evanston, Illinois, Hospital.

"We started the study to establish that Lamaze childbirth isn't harmful; instead we found that it is very beneficial," said Dr. Michael Hughey, who headed the study. The research compared the childbirth of 500 Lamaze-trained women with 500 without the training.

The Lamaze-prepared women had one-fourth as many caesarean section deliveries as did the other women and only one-fifth of their babies had fetal distress.

The death rate among babies born to Lamaze-trained women was one-fourth the death rate of those born to women without the training.

The non-Lamaze group also had three times as much toxemia of pregnancy and twice as many premature deliveries as did the Lamaze group.

---

*Reprinted, courtesy of the Chicago *Tribune*.

Lamaze training emphasizes proper breathing for pregnant women, teaches them how to relax, deal with stress.

"I don't know why the Lamaze group did better than the control group, but the data were overwhelming," Dr. Hughey said.

He speculated that women who choose to take Lamaze training may have an above average interest in having a good pregnancy and that their positive mental attitude may benefit them.

Dr. Thomas McElin of Evanston Hospital and Todd Young worked with Dr. Hughey on the study. The study was published in the Journal of the American College of Obstretricians and Gynecologists.

From the Santa Ana *Register*
Tuesday, June 20, 1978

What makes a good childbirth class?

1. We suggest that you find one that teaches the original, "pure" Lamaze techniques. Many people teach "modified" techniques, methods by other names, or a combination of methods, but couples are still more highly satisfied when they learn the Lamaze method *totally.* It should go without saying that classes on hospital procedures and baby care do not usually fall into the "pure Lamaze" category.

2. A private instructor, not salaried by any doctor or hospital, will be more likely to give an objective view of available options in your area.

3. The instructor must have experienced a Lamaze birth *herself.* She need not be a nurse, but she must know from experience that the method works. She should have been through a specialized training program and should have contact with, and knowledge of, the local medical community.

4. The course should be at least six weeks in length, preferably more.

5. The classes should be small—no more than ten couples (fewer than ten is even better).

6. The fee should be reasonable. Try not to make cost the deciding factor, since it has *no* bearing on the quality of the class. Some good classess are still very inexpensive, and some very poor classes have a high price tag.

7. The teacher should have a lending library of pertinent reading materials available to her students.

8. She should offer, in addition to labor-delivery information and breathing techniques, sound advice on nutrition, breast-feeding, postpartum, and baby care.

9. Most important of all, you should "like her" before you ever meet her. If she is friendly, enthusiastic, and helpful over the phone, she will be that way in class, too.

WORKING TOGETHER

The Third Trimester

1. What were your emotions when you first felt the baby's movements?

2. How do you think your priorities in life might change after you become a mother or father?

3. Do babies have emotional needs? If so, what are they and how do you hope to meet your baby's needs?

4. Name five qualities you see in your mate that will make him or her a good parent.

CHAPTER 2

Why Prepare for Childbirth?

Prepare thine heart, and stretch out thine hands toward him.
(Job 11:13)

As the creator of all life, God designed women's bodies in such a way that under normal conditions they function correctly. Otherwise the human race would have disappeared long ago. If you believe that your body is "wonderfully made," you must also believe that under normal circumstances, you are able to give birth comfortably and with joy, and that this is God's will for you!

"But what about the 'curse'? How can I give birth without pain when God told Eve we must suffer?" women ask. Our answer to this is found in God's Word itself, with comments by two authorities.

Dr. Ed Wheat emphasizes that women are *not* cursed. Neither are men. If you look closely at Genesis 3:17 you will see that it was the *ground* God cursed. This was done for the benefit of fallen mankind—to give people work to do, since no one is truly happy in a state of idleness. In Proverbs 14:23 we are told that "in all labour there is profit." The Hebrew root word for "labor" in that verse (*etsev*) is the same word used to describe the work man exerts in "subduing the earth" and the effort women put forth bearing children. The word *etsev* refers to strenuous, intense toil or hard work, but *not necessarily pain.*

Unfortunately, many translators have assigned different meanings to the same root word:

> *To the woman he said, I will greatly multiply your pain* [etsev] *in childbearing; in pain* [etsev] *you shall bring forth children. . . .And to Adam he said, . . . cursed is the ground because*

of you; in toil [etsev] *you shall eat of it all the days of your life.*
(Gen. 3:16, 17, RSV)

God was, in reality, establishing a system whereby man could live most effectively in a sin-tainted world—a system that, when followed, causes the "curse" to have no effect on us. This system includes, not pain in childbirth as many would have us believe, but toil—LABOR—climaxed with indescribable satisfaction and unspeakable joy. And the latter part of Genesis 3:16 explicitly describes how this labor is to be carried out: " . . . thy desire shall be to thy husband, and *he shall rule over thee.*"

It is not surprising, then, that methods of husband-coached childbirth are so effective. Although their originators did not realize it, the discovery that the husband's presence and encouragement relieved pain in labor was actually the *re*discovery of a law of nature, set forth in Genesis.[1]

Prepared childbirth can be considered a perfect fulfilllment of God's plan for your marriage. Through it, husband and wife *labor together* as one flesh, the way God intended. If the wife follows her husband's directives and allows him to "rule" over her, the work they do together will be neither grievous nor painful.

Another source of extensive research on this subject is *The Joy of Natural Childbirth* by Helen Wessel. This book is the result of a detailed study of all biblical passages relating to pain in childbearing. It is interesting—and comforting—to know that, when traced back to the original languages, all words which have been translated to indicate "pain" are used elsewhere in Scripture to mean hard work, patient waiting, groans of pleasure, and cries of joy.[2]

There is something to be said, too, for the idea that a woman's toil brings "sorrow," not with the pregnancy or birth of a child, but in the experience of motherhood itself. Who else feels the bonds of love or the pangs of separation, or the physical or emotional pain a child goes through more strongly than his own mother? This attachment to one's child is a unique phenomenon that only a mother can adequately describe. It is obvious that God intended a special relationship to exist between mother and child. These days that relationship is called "bonding."

THE TIES THAT BIND

That ye may suck, and be satisfied with the breasts of her consolations. . . . Ye shall be born upon her sides, and be dandled upon her knees. As one whom his mother comforteth, so will I comfort you . . . your heart shall rejoice, and your bones shall flourish. (Isa. 66:11-14)

A bond is a strong tie between two people, and "bonding" is the formation of the very first love-ties between the baby and his family. Bonding begins in pregnancy. It reaches its peak in the interaction of mother and child shortly after birth. And it lasts a lifetime. It is the touching and caressing, the complex exchange of looks, sounds, affectionate gestures, and even smells. It is a mother talking with her baby, cooing over him, getting to know him. It is the most natural thing in the world. What mother doesn't want to hold close, at the moment of birth, that warm, inviting bundle of life that has been a part of her for nine months?

We were designed to "bond." If a mother is awake for the birth of her child, and is allowed to freely hold and interact with the infant immediately, the bonding will take place—no great fanfare, just the beginning of a relationship of deep, immeasurable love.

The Bible contains several striking examples of women who were obviously bonded to their infants.

Hannah was a godly woman who dedicated her son to the Lord, even before he was conceived. But she was also aware of God's plan for children to have a mother physically present, and she was "tuned in" to Samuel's need for her. She did not allow herself to be separated from him until she was certain that he was ready. She was undoubtedly bonded to her baby.

An even more impressive biblical example of the importance of bonding is the case of Solomon—one of the wisest men in history—using the mother-child bond as a test to discern which of two women was the *real* mother of a certain baby.

Two women who lived in the same house each gave birth to baby boys, three days apart. Shortly thereafter, one of the babies died in its sleep. The mother of the dead infant tried to switch babies and convince the other woman that it was *her* child that had died. They finally took their dispute to King Solomon, who provided a wise solution. He called for a sword and said, "Divide the living child in two, and give half to the one and half to the other." One woman begged, "Give her [the other woman] the living child, and in no wise slay it." The Bible says, "Her heart yearned over her son" (RSV), but the other woman responded with, "Let it be neither mine nor thine, but divide it" (1 Kings 3:26).

Solomon immediately discerned who the real mother was, just by her desire to see the child live. He ordered his servants to give the child to her.

Although it has not been called such, "bonding" has been practiced since the beginning of humanity. Only in the past half-century, with the use of anesthesia in childbirth, have drugged infants been pulled from their groggy mothers and immediately removed to a nursery so both child and mother could recover—which they needed to do! The first face-to-face meeting of the two was many hours, sometimes days, later; and often, the longer the delay, the less interested either party was in the meeting. Soul-to-soul communication between mother and newborn at birth was made not only unlikely but practically impossible.

Today, however, childbirth is being steered down more family-centered avenues, and parents are realizing the value of early and continuous contact with their babies. New methods of preparation which minimize the need for medication, as well as more relaxed hospital policies and procedures, make this possible.

Most theories of bonding have been adopted from observation of the animal kingdom. Researchers Klaus and Kennell consider the process similar to "imprinting" found in baby geese, where they become attached to and tirelessly follow the first moving object they see after birth, whether it be their mother or the mailman. Other studies have shown that if a goat's kid is removed from the mother's presence immediately after birth and reintroduced an hour later, the mother will reject it. But if mother and kid are given five minutes together before the separation, the mother will accept and care for the kid when it is returned.

In a recent article, however, Dr. Klaus noted that humans are actually quite different from other members of the animal kingdom. (We knew that all along!) With humans, the "attachment process" actually begins in pregnancy, with the first fetal movements, and continues into the first three days postpartum. If mothers are capable of, and allowed, unlimited contact with their infants during the first three days of the postpartum period, their mothering behavior has been shown to be superior after one month, and even after a year compared to mothers who did not have unlimited contact. They were more capable of soothing their children and more reluctant to leave them. They also held and carried their children more, and were more openly affectionate. At two years of age, their babies were surprisingly more advanced verbally than those who had not received the extra contact at birth.

Dr. Klaus suggests that we should begin to think of the attachment process in terms similar to those which describe the first breathing efforts by the baby; since breathing is such a vital and life-sustaining force, the first breaths a baby takes are not triggered by only one factor. If that were the case, failure of that single factor to operate would end the baby's life. Instead, *several* things influence the baby to take its first breath, and if one fails, the others continue the effort. Bonding is now being recognized as an equally life-sustaining force, and it is felt that it is probably instigated at several points during the first three days after birth, rather than just one "critical period."[3] This is certainly logical, for we have seen mothers who, for one reason or another, were unable to see and hold their babies immediately after birth; in spite of this, they have a very good relationship with the child and are very good mothers.

There are many things you can plan in regard to your birth experience which will increase your chances for early contact with the baby and maximize the effects of bonding. Investigate the alternative labor, delivery, and postpartum practices your hospital offers. Following are some practices which are gaining popularity:

Unmedicated birth—The use of prepared childbirth breathing and relaxation techniques, whenever possible, will guarantee that both mother and baby are mentally alert and ready for immediate closeness.

Demand feeding—Your baby is brought to you when he cries to be fed or when you want to feed him, rather than at the traditional four-hour intervals.

Rooming in—Your baby actually stays in your room and is cared for by you! Most hospitals offer a modified type of rooming-in, in which the baby is moved to the nursery when the mother requests, and also during the night, while she sleeps. Ideally, at night the baby is brought back "on demand," or at least at four-hour intervals.

Fathers' visiting hours—These provide time for extended contact between father and baby, and allow them to be bonded in their own special way.

Sibling visitation—The rules for this vary from place to place, but generally it provides an opportunity for the older brothers and sisters to look at, and possibly touch, the baby and to develop a sibling "bond." It also reassures them that Mommy and baby are all right and that the family is still a unit.

Alternative birth rooms or labor room deliveries—These allow for a more relaxed and homelike, less "hospitalized" delivery. Usually both parents and the baby are allowed to remain together after the birth to enjoy each other and become acquainted.

Early discharge—This practice allows mother and baby to leave the hospital anywhere from two to twenty-four hours after the birth, and return to the relaxing and loving surroundings of their own home. For getting acquainted with a new family member, "there's no place like home!"

Birth centers—Almost a "cross" between a hospital and a doctor's office, these facilities are found in increasing numbers across America. Usually run by doctors or nurse-midwives, they offer the comforts of a home, the safety of a medical backup, and the joy of a very personally tailored birth experience.

Nurse-midwife delivery—Some hospitals now offer programs in which the baby is delivered by a certified nurse-midwife. The nurse-midwife also conducts most of the prenatal examinations as well as the postpartum check-up. A nurse-midwife will usually spend more time with the mother during labor than a doctor would, and the delivery fee is generally lower. The title nurse-midwife should not be confused with that of lay-midwife; lay-midwives cannot practice legally in many states.

Remember that no matter how many alternatives a hospital offers, you are likely to wish you could have more contact with your baby than you actually receive. Our advice here is to take advantage of every opportunity, then grin and bear the rest. When you get home (and we hope it will be soon!), you can hold and cuddle your baby as much as you want!

A MOTHER'S BIRTH REPORT*

Both my husband and I were interested in natural childbirth classes because we had heard so many good things about them. My doctor was also in favor of this type of birth. Chuck and I attended classes and awaited the exciting day.

The first indication of my labor came after I had prayed that I might have my baby soon, that I couldn't wait much longer. Late Saturday night I felt a little cramp. Soon after, I noticed a bit of spotting on my nightgown. I went to sleep but was awakened twice during the night by a backache. Early Sunday morning I lost the mucus plug. I phoned my doctor immediately. He told me to take it easy, but to time my contractions and call him when they were ten minutes apart. When I told my husband what was happening, he could hardly believe it was time to become a daddy—a time which he was awaiting eagerly. We decided to go over to my parents' house because it was much closer to the hospital. On the way I had two contractions in the car and they were about thirty minutes apart.

I did not contact my doctor until the contractions were about ten minutes apart—around 3:00 in the afternoon. During each contraction I got in the pelvic rock position and had Chuck rub my back. Soon, the intervals between my contractions decreased from ten minutes to five minutes. We phoned the doctor and told him we'd meet him at the hospital. I had two more contractions on the way to the hospital. They were much closer together but not any stronger. I used slow, deep chest breathing the entire time and was very relaxed during the contractions. At 4:00 we arrived at the hospital; the nurse checked me and announced I had dilated to five centimeters. I had previously made sure that I would not be prepped or given an enema. The doctor came in

---

*Used by permission of Diane Vidal.

about ten minutes later and broke the bag of waters. He said I was at eight centimeters and decided not to use the internal fetal monitor because I was ready to give birth any minute.

I was wheeled into the delivery room by my nurse. Chuck and the doctor changed their clothes. In the delivery room my husband stood by my side holding my hand and praising me the entire time. My nurse was very kind and encouraging. My doctor assured me I was doing well and I would not need any medication. I became more confident after hearing that. We were all relaxed and working hard together. I began pushing; after about three pushes I got the hang of it and decided to give it all I had. With one more push our son Joey was born. I felt great the entire time. While my husband checked the baby, the doctor repaired a tiny tear. I had done well without an episiotomy.

We were now a family of three. Chuck and I were in tears watching our miracle begin his life. Thank you, my husband! You'll never know how much you helped to make it easier for me. I had never realized that both the father and the mother go through all the contractions and, better yet, the birth, together!

PART II

EVERYTHING YOU ALWAYS WANTED TO KNOW ABOUT CHILDBIRTH BUT DIDN'T KNOW WHOM TO ASK!

We have already stressed the necessity of enrollment in a good series of childbirth preparation classes.

The following section is based on the student manual used in classes conducted by Genesia Childbirth Educators. If you attend classes other than ours, we trust you will still find this portion helpful in reinforcing what you learn from your instructor.

The lessons are designed to be studied and practiced over a seven-week period, one lesson per week.

CHAPTER 3

Let's Get Started

As thou knowest not . . . how the bones grow in the womb of her that is with child, even so thou knowest not the works of God, who maketh all. (Eccles. 11:5)

Bless the Lord, O my soul, and forget not all his benefits: who satisfieth thy mouth with good things, so that thy youth is renewed. . . . (Ps. 103:2, 5)

We are what we eat! All parents want a baby that is in good health, free from birth defects, illness, or brain damage. What many parents may *not* know is that the mother's diet and personal habits during pregnancy are the major factors which determine the health of that child.

Most women believe that they eat well; after all, most of us don't appear to be starving. However, during pregnancy it is very easy to become deficient in one or several essential nutrients if an adequate diet is not maintained.

Take a minute right now and write down everything you have eaten or drunk in the past twenty-four hours. Now compare it with the diet guide below, which lists the necessary amounts of food a woman must eat to nourish herself and the baby adequately.

DAILY DIET GUIDE FOR PREGNANT WOMEN

Each day consume:

3-4 cups milk	2 servings (2 oz. each) lean meat, fish, or poultry	4-6 vegetables, fresh or frozen
1 egg		
3-5 fresh fruits		3-4 servings WHOLE GRAIN foods
	1 tbsp. fat	

How well did you do? The main area in which expectant mothers short themselves is that of protein-rich foods (meat, fish, poultry, eggs, milk, cheese, and other dairy products; also beans, lentils, grains, and rice in combinations). A pregnant woman's protein requirement soars to between 80 and 100 grams a day—about two to three times as much as you are used to eating ordinarily. The most important function of the protein you eat is that of building the brain cells of your unborn child. The quality and quantity of these cells help determine your child's future I.Q.

God planned for people to eat foods the way He created them—not processed, refined, degerminated, and stripped of every health-building component. Women who eat foods that are as natural as possible, and in quantities that satisfy their hunger, will have exceptionally bright, healthy and strong babies.

Current research indicates that women should not restrict their weight gain during pregnancy, even if they are overweight to begin with. If a woman is eating according to appetite, and choosing *only* from a variety of natural foods, she will gain, on the average, 30 pounds, all of which can be lost after delivery if she breastfeeds her baby. It has been proven that mothers who gain 24-30 pounds during pregnancy have healthier babies, while mothers who restrict their food intake are more prone to miscarriage, premature labor, toxemia, and other pregnancy complications. But the biggest danger is to their babies, who have a far higher incidence of low birth weight, prematurity, stillbirth, brain damage, respiratory distress, retarded development, epilepsy, and other problems.

Over-the-counter drugs, even as common as pain relief medications and cold capsules, should be avoided, as their effect on the unborn is not known. And smoking and drinking, even in very slight to moderate amounts, have been proven to cause damage to the baby in every medical study conducted.

It is *never too late* to correct poor nutritional habits. Begin TODAY for a better TOMORROW. Using the list of foods and the sample chart on the following pages, record and analyze the quality of your diet. Then you'll know exactly what you must do to change your eating habits.

PROTEIN AND CALORIE CONTENT OF
SOME COMMON PROTEIN FOODS[1]

	Food	Portion Size	Calories	Protein (Grams)
Cereals	All-Bran	⅓ c.	70	3
	Cheerios	1 c.	102	3.4
	cornflakes	1 c.	95	2.1
	cream of wheat, cooked	1 c.	130	4.4
	oatmeal, cooked	1 c.	148	5.4
	Quaker 100% natural	⅓ c.	186	5.3
	Special K	1 c.	60	3.2
	Sugar Crisp	1 c.	126	2.3
	wheat germ	¼ c.	103	7.5
	Wheaties	1 c.	104	2.8
Dairy Products and Eggs	eggs, large	1 egg	88	7.0
	cottage cheese	½ c.	120	15.3
	natural cheddar cheese	1 oz.	115	7.2
	natural Swiss cheese	1 oz.	106	7.7
	process American cheese	1 oz.	107	6.5
	milk, whole, fresh	1 c.	162	8.6
	nonfat dry milk solids	1 c.	215	21.4
	ice cream	⅙ qt.	186	3.6
	ice milk	⅙ qt.	137	4.3
	yogurt, from skim milk	1 c.	122	8.3
	yogurt, from whole milk	1 c.	151	7.3
Flours	soy, low fat	1 c.	356	43.4
	white, all-purpose	1 c.	400	11.6
	whole wheat	1 c.	400	16.0
	rye	1 c.	268	7.5
Grains and Pasta	barley, pearled, dry	¼ c.	196	4.6
	cornmeal, dry	¼ c.	135	2.9
	rice, white, dry	¼ c.	178	3.3
	rice, brown, dry	¼ c.	176	3.7
	egg noodles, dry	¼ c.	70	2.3
	macaroni, dry	¼ c.	101	3.4
	spaghetti, dry	¼ c.	140	4.8
Legumes	kidney beans, dry	½ c.	343	22.5
	lentils, dry	½ c.	340	24.7
	limas, dry	½ c.	345	20.4
	navy beans, dry	½ c.	345	20.4
	split peas, dry	½ c.	348	24.2
	peanut butter	1 T.	86	3.9
	peanuts, shelled	1 T.	86	4.0

	soybeans, dry	½ c.	403	34.1
	soybeans, immature, cooked	½ c.	88	7.4
	soybeans, mature, cooked	½ c.	130	11.0
Meats and fish	beef:			
	ground beef	¼ lb. raw	304	20.3
	ground beef, lean	¼ lb. raw	203	23.4
	chuck roast, choice	¼ lb. raw	337	15.5
	chuck roast, good	¼ lb. raw	288	16.7
	sirloin steak, choice	¼ lb. raw	229	17.8
	round steak, choice	¼ lb. raw	216	22.1
	chicken, fryers:			
	whole, ready-to-cook	½ lb. raw	191	28.7
	breasts	½ lb. raw	197	37.3
	drumsticks	½ lb. raw	157	25.6
	thighs	½ lb. raw	218	30.8
	fish:			
	cod, flesh only	¼ lb. raw	89	20.0
	flounder, flesh only	¼ lb. raw	90	19.0
	haddock, flesh only	¼ lb. raw	89	20.8
	mackerel, canned	¼ lb.	208	21.9
	perch, flesh only	¼ lb. raw	108	21.6
	salmon, canned	¼ lb.	160	27.0
	tuna, canned in water	¼ lb.	144	32.0
	pork:			
	bacon	¼ lb. raw	667	9.3
	ham, picnic	¼ lb. raw	265	15.6
	ham, canned, boneless	¼ lb.	189	20.9
	loin chops	¼ lb. raw	266	15.3
	sausage, links or bulk	¼ lb. raw	565	10.7
	miscellaneous meats:			
	bologna	¼ lb.	345	13.7
	frankfurters, all meat	¼ lb.	361	14.9
	luncheon meat, canned	¼ lb.	334	17.0
	salami	¼ lb.	352	19.9
	scrapple	¼ lb.	194	10.0
	beef liver	¼ lb. raw	159	22.6
	chicken livers	¼ lb. raw	146	22.4

PC = Protein Count

KEEP TRACK OF WHAT YOU EAT

Meal	Monday Food	PC	Tuesday Food	PC	Wednesday Food	PC	Thursday Food	PC	Friday Food	PC	Saturday Food	PC	Sunday Food	PC
Breakfast														
Morning Snack														
Lunch														
Afternoon Snack														
Dinner														
Evening Snack														
Protein Total														
Circle servings in each group	Milk 1 1 1 1 Egg 1 Fruit 1 1 1 1 1 Veg. 1 1 1 1 1 Protein 1 1 Grains 1 1 1 1 Fat 1		Milk 1 1 1 1 Egg 1 Fruit 1 1 1 1 1 Veg. 1 1 1 1 1 Protein 1 1 Grains 1 1 1 1 Fat 1		Milk 1 1 1 1 Egg 1 Fruit 1 1 1 1 1 Veg. 1 1 1 1 1 Protein 1 1 Grains 1 1 1 1 Fat 1		Milk 1 1 1 1 Egg 1 Fruit 1 1 1 1 1 Veg. 1 1 1 1 1 Protein 1 1 Grains 1 1 1 1 Fat 1		Milk 1 1 1 1 Egg 1 Fruit 1 1 1 1 1 Veg. 1 1 1 1 1 Protein 1 1 Grains 1 1 1 1 Fat 1		Milk 1 1 1 1 Egg 1 Fruit 1 1 1 1 1 Veg. 1 1 1 1 1 Protein 1 1 Grains 1 1 1 1 Fat 1		Milk 1 1 1 1 Egg 1 Fruit 1 1 1 1 1 Veg. 1 1 1 1 1 Protein 1 1 Grains 1 1 1 1 Fat 1	

ARE YOU READY?

To have truly satisfying pregnancy, birth, and parenting experiences, a great deal of planning and forethought are necessary. Here are some suggestions to help make yours the very best experiences possible.

A satisfying pregnancy is one in which you "feel good" physically, emotionally, and spiritually.

1. You need plenty of rest, exercise, and good nutrition on a daily basis.
2. Plan special "quality" time with your family. Strive to know and love each member of the family in a deeper way.
3. It is only natural, as you become a partaker in God's creative nature, that you desire to know your Maker better. Satisfy this desire by drawing closer to God in prayer.

A satisfying birth is one in which you understand what is happening and have planned accordingly down to the last detail:

1. Most of the knowledge you need will come from childbirth classes and books. From these sources you will get ideas on how to handle your labor.
2. Take a tour of the hospital (or an objective look at your home, in the case of a home birth). This will help make your plans more detailed.
3. Discuss your plans with your doctor. Remember that what you want is not always what you get, unless you have reached an agreement in advance with your doctor. (See "Communicating with Your Doctor." p. 57.)
4. Imagine you are leaving for the hospital. What if the sitter for your other children is not available? Will you be comfortable in the front seat of the car, or should you take along extra pillows and a blanket and ride in the back? Think through your departure and you will reduce last-minute confusion.

Satisfying early parenting is an anxiety-free time in which you are free from all responsibilities other than the care of your new baby.

1. Learn how to breastfeed so you can reduce those early anxieties. While breastfeeding is a *natural* function, most women have not been informed enough to learn the tech-

niques. You can learn by reading and by attending La Leche League meetings (address, p. 183).

2. Know how to take care of your new baby; you will avoid many fears and worries common to new parents. You can learn by reading parenting and child-care books, or by attending baby-care classes (not to be confused with childbirth classes). These are offered by the Red Cross, as well as many hospitals.

3. Put your household in order, thus easing the family's readjustment period considerably. Arrange for someone to help around the house; prepare and freeze some meals; and stock up on disposable diapers for the first few weeks.

THE PREGNANT PATIENT'S BILL OF RIGHTS

American parents are becoming increasingly aware that well-intentioned health professionals do not always have scientific data to support common American obstetrical practices and that many of these practices are carried out primarily because they are part of medical and hospital tradition. In the last forty years many artificial practices have been introduced which have changed childbirth from a physiological event to a very complicated medical procedure in which all kinds of drugs are used and procedures carried out, sometimes unnecessarily, and many of them potentially damaging for the baby and even for the mother. A growing body of research makes it alarmingly clear that every aspect of traditional American hospital care during labor and delivery must now be questioned as to its possible effect on the future well-being of both the obstetric patient and her unborn child.

One in every 35 children born in the United States today will eventually be diagnosed as retarded; in 75% of these cases there is no familiar or genetic predisposing factor. One in every 10 to 17 children has been found to have some form of brain dysfunction or learning disability requiring special treatment. Such statistics are not confined to the lower socioeconomic group but cut across all segments of American society.

New concerns are being raised by childbearing women because no one knows what degree of oxygen depletion, head compression, or traction by forceps the unborn or newborn infant can tolerate before that child sustains permanent brain damage or dysfunction. The recent findings regarding the cancer-related drug diethylstilbestrol have alerted the public to the fact that neither the approval of a drug by the U.S. Food and Drug Administration nor the fact that a drug is prescribed by a physician serves as a guarantee that a drug or medication is safe for the mother or her unborn child. In fact, the American Academy of Pediatrics' Committee on Drugs has recently stated that there is no drug, whether prescription or over-the-counter remedy, which has been proven save for the unborn child.

The Pregnant Patient has the right to participate in decisions involving her well-being and that of her unborn child, unless there is a clearcut medical emergency that prevents her participation. In addition to the rights set forth in the American Hospital Association's "Patient's Bill of Rights" (which has also been adopted by the New York City Department of Health), the Pregnant Patient, because she represents TWO patients rather than one, should be recognized as having the additional rights listed below.

1. *The Pregnant Patient has the right*, prior to the administration of any drug or procedure, to be informed by the health professional caring for her of any potential direct or indirect effects, risks or hazards to herself or her unborn or newborn infant which may result from the use of a drug or procedure prescribed for or administered to her during pregnancy, labor, birth or lactation.

2. *The Pregnant Patient has the right*, prior to the proposed therapy, to be informed, not only of the benefits, risks and hazards of the proposed therapy but also of known alternative therapy, such as available childbirth education classes which could help to prepare the Pregnant Patient physically and mentally to cope with the discomfort or stress of pregnancy and the experience of childbirth, thereby reducing or eliminating her need for drugs and obstretic intervention. She should be offered such information early in her pregnancy in order that she may make a reasoned decision.

3. *The Pregnant Patient has the right*, prior to the administration of any drug, to be informed by the health professional

who is prescribing or administering the drug to her that any drug she receives during pregnancy, labor and birth, no matter how or when the drug is taken or administered, may adversely affect her unborn baby, directly or indirectly, and that there is no drug or chemical which has been proven safe for the unborn child.

4. *The Pregnant Patient has the right,* if cesarean birth is anticipated, to be informed prior to the administration of any drug, and preferably prior to her hospitalization, that minimizing her and, in turn, her baby's intake of nonessential pre-operative medicine will benefit her baby.

5. *The Pregnant Patient has the right*, prior to the administration of a drug or procedure, to be informed of the areas of uncertainty if there is NO properly controlled follow-up research which has established the safety of the drug or procedure with regard to its direct and/or indirect effects on the physiological, mental and neurological development of the child exposed, via the mother, to the drug or procedure during pregnancy, labor, birth or lactation (this would apply to virtually all drugs and the vast majority of obstetric procedures).

6. *The Pregnant Patient has the right*, prior to the administration of any drug, to be informed of the brand name and generic name of the drug in order that she may advise the health professional of any past adverse reaction to the drug.

7. *The Pregnant Patient has the right* to determine for herself, without pressure from her attendant, whether she will accept the risks inherent in the proposed therapy or refuse a drug or procedure.

8. *The Pregnant Patient has the right* to know the name and qualifications of the individual administering a medication or procedure to her during labor or birth.

9. *The Pregnant Patient has the right* to be informed, prior to the administration of any procedure, whether that procedure is being administered to her for her or her baby's benefit (medically indicated) or as an elective procedure (for convenience, teaching purposes or research).

10. *The Pregnant Patient has the right* to be accompanied during the stress of labor and birth by someone else she cares for, and to whom she looks for emotional comfort and encouragement.

11. *The Pregnant Patient has the right* after appropriate medical consultation to choose a position for labor and for birth which is least stressful to her baby and to herself.

12. *The Obstetric Patient has the right* to have her baby cared for at her bedside if her baby is normal, and to feed her baby according to her baby's needs rather than according to the hospital regimen.

13. *The Obstetric Patient has the right* to be informed in writing of the name of the person who actually delivered her baby and the professional qualifications of that person. This information should also be on the birth certificate.

14. *The Obstetric Patient has the right* to be informed if there is any known or indicated aspect of her or her baby's care or condition which may cause her or her baby later difficulty or problems.

15. *The Obstetric Patient has the right* to have her and her baby's hospital medical records complete, accurate and legible and to have their records, including Nurses' Notes, retained by the hospital until the child reaches at least the age of majority, or, alternately, to have the records offered to her before they are destroyed.

16. *The Obstetric Patient*, both during and after her hospital stay, has the right to have access to her complete hospital medical records, including Nurses' Notes, and to receive a copy upon payment of a reasonable fee and without incurring the expense of retaining an attorney.

It is the obstetric patient and her baby, not the health professional, who must sustain any trauma or injury resulting from the use of a drug or obstetric procedure. The observation of the rights listed above will not only permit the obstetric patient to participate in the decisions involving her and her baby's health care, but will help to protect the health professional and the hospital against litigation arising from resentment or misunderstanding on the part of the mother.

Prepared by Doris Haire, Chair., ICEA Committee on Health Law and Regulation. Reprinted by permission of ICEA.

THE PREGNANT PATIENT'S RESPONSIBILITIES

In addition to understanding her rights, the Pregnant Patient should also understand that she too has certain responsibilities. The Pregnant Patient's responsibilities include the following:

1. The Pregnant Patient is responsible for learning about the physical and psychological process of labor, birth and postpartum recovery. The better informed expectant parents are the better they will be able to participate in decisions concerning the planning of their care.

2. The Pregnant Patient is responsible for learning what comprises good prenatal and intranatal care and for making an effort to obtain the best care possible.

3. Expectant parents are responsible for knowing about those hospital policies and regulations which will affect their birth and postpartum experience.

4. The Pregnant Patient is responsible for arranging for a companion or support person (husband, mother, sister, friend, etc.) who will share in her plans for birth and who will accompany her during her labor and birth experience.

5. The Pregnant patient is responsible for making her preferences known clearly to the health professionals involved in her case in a courteous and cooperative manner and for making mutually agreed-upon arrangements regarding maternity care alternatives with her physician and hospital in advance of labor.

6. Expectant parents are responsible for listening to their chosen physician or midwife with an open mind, just as they expect him or her to listen openly to them.

7. Once they have agreed to a course of health care, expectant parents are responsible, to the best of their ability, for seeing that the program is carried out in consultation with others with whom they have made the agreement.

8. The Pregnant Patient is responsible for obtaining information in advance regarding the approximate cost of her obstetric and hospital care.

9. The Pregnant Patient who intends to change her physician or hospital is responsible for notifying all concerned, well in advance of the birth if possible, and for informing both of her reasons for changing.

10. In all their interactions with medical and nursing personnel, the expectant parents should behave towards those caring for them with the same respect and consideration they themselves would like.

11. During the mother's hospital stay the mother is responsible for learning about her and her baby's continuing care after discharge from the hospital.

12. After birth, the parents should put into writing constructive comments and feelings of satisfaction and/or dissatisfaction with the care (nursing, medical and personal) they received. Good service to families in the future will be facilitated by those parents who take the time and responsibility to write letters expressing their feelings about the maternity care they received.

All the previous statements assume a normal birth and postpartum experience. Expectant parents should realize that, if complications develop in their cases, there will be an increased need to trust the expertise of the physician and hospital staff they have chosen. However, if problems occur, the childbearing woman still retains her responsibility for making informed decisions about her care or treatment and that of her baby. If she is incapable of assuming that responsibility because of her physical condition, her previously authorized companion or support person should assume responsibility for making informed decisions on her behalf.

Prepared by Members of ICEA. Published by International Childbirth Education Association, Inc. Reprinted by permission of ICEA.

Thoughts on Home Birth

A growing number of couples are choosing to have their babies at home rather than in a hospital. It is not our purpose to persuade couples to choose one place of delivery over another, but to prepare them for whatever manner of birth experience they have chosen. Couples who decide to deliver their babies at home must make safety a major concern. For this reason, we give the following guidelines:

1. Good health is the first prerequisite for having a safe home birth. You should feel great; this requires plenty of exercise, a superior diet and a physique that is conducive to a normal labor.

2. Your age and the number of pregnancies you have had affect the safety in a home birth. Generally, women between seventeen and forty years of age are not considered overly high risks for home birth. But, this is only true in the light of the number of pregnancies you have had—the more pregnancies, the greater your chances of complications.

3. From all indications the baby should be normal and give no reason for concern that the birth would be anything but average. (This rules out such cases as prematurity, postmaturity, multiple births and unfavorable presentations.)

4. Breastfeeding is essential in a home birth. Breastfeeding helps the baby adjust to his new environment. It also keeps the mother's uterus contracted, preventing excessive bleeding.

5. We cannot stress enough the importance of receiving quality prenatal care and obtaining competent medical assistance for

the birth. Good prenatal care should start early in the pregnancy. It provides good insurance against complications. If problems do arise, they can be detected early enough to correct. Thus, both the baby and mother are protected.

6. Both parents need to be educated in all aspects of birth and home delivery. They need to spend time together planning and preparing for the birth-day. Lester Hazell notes, in her book *Commonsense Childbirth*:

> A couple who is not meshing well psychologically tends to produce a labor which doesn't mesh well physically. . . . Both members need to realize that each is totally responsible to themselves, each other, and their child.[2]

Practical Lesson 1

POSITIONS FOR LABOR AND EXERCISES

Semi-Supine Position. Lie down with your back elevated at a 45° angle. Have knees bent and supported with pillows.

Side Position. Lie on your side with upper knee bent and supported with a pillow. It may be more comfortable to have a pillow running lengthwise from your head to your chest and cradled between your breasts. This takes most of the pressure off sore breasts.

Tailor-Sitting Position. Sit up with your legs crossed "Indian style" and your shoulders slightly rounded. This takes the contracting uterus off your back and allows gravity to work with your contractions.

Tailor-Sitting (as an exercise). This stretches the muscles of your perineum and inner thighs. If your thigh muscles stretch comfortably, you will be far more comfortable with your legs spread for the birth of your baby. Sitting in this position each day may reduce back discomfort during pregnancy and reduce the need for an episiotomy in labor.

Butterfly. This is a variation of tailor-sitting. Sitting with the soles of your feet touching, pull your heels to your pubis and push down on your knees. Bounce knees several times.

Pelvic Rock. This eases back discomfort, leg pain, or pressure on nerves in the pelvic area. It raises the uterus into its proper position, relieving the stress on the back. Start on hands and knees with knees slightly apart and arms wide apart. Arch your back like a cat, then sink down to form a concave curve. Repeat this flexing motion twenty times, twice a day. This can also be done in knee-chest position, standing, and, with the aid of the coach, a side position.

Expressing Complementary Air. This strengthens the diaphragm—the muscles you will use for pushing the baby out. Inhale deeply through the nose, then exhale slowly through the mouth with slightly pursed lips. When you run out of air, blow out five more seconds. You should feel your abdominal muscles tighten all the way around to your sides.

Kegel Exercises

The pelvic floor is a group of muscles (called pubococcygeus) which support the rectum, urethra, bladder, and internal reproductive organs. It is important for these muscles to be strengthened in order to minimize injury and discomfort during the birth of your baby.

Dr. Arnold H. Kegel (who developed this exercise) found that toning the pelvic floor before and after birth can also eliminate such problems as prolapsed uterus, cystocele, and rectocele. Sexual enjoyment will be increased with improved muscle tone also.

Kegel Step 1. Contract and release the pelvic floor muscles while you are on the toilet. Try to urinate by the teaspoonful. Contract and release strongly and quickly to stop and release the flow. This exercise can be done at other times during the day also—while washing dishes, standing in lines, driving the car, or just sitting around. Do at least 75 Kegels a day from now on.

Neuromuscular Release. Of all prepared childbirth techniques, the most important during labor is conscious release. The normal reaction to the contraction of the uterus is tensing up. You need to learn to release and eliminate this tension consciously in order to cope with labor in a positive manner. To control the various muscles of your body you must first learn to identify and differentiate them:

1. Get into a comfortable position and go limp. Now *slowly* tense your right hand. Move the tension slowly up your forearm and then your upper arm. Notice what the muscles feel like as they tighten. *Slowly* "let go" of the tension in your upper arm. Let it drain down the forearm, through the hand, and out your fingers.

2. Now do the same thing with your left arm, then one leg at

a time, your chest and shoulders, your face and neck, and lastly, the muscles of the pelvic floor. Take time to really concentrate on the sensations.

You should gain control well enough to be able to relax any part of your body that your husband touches (as in photo).

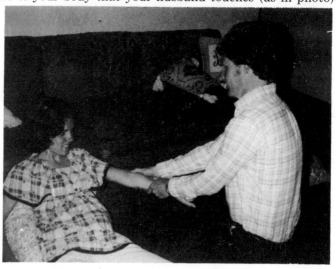

A Word About Practice . . . PRACTICE!

You should begin working together in daily sessions *this week.* Although there is not yet much to do together, it is important that you establish the habit of setting aside time each day to rehearse for labor.

Chapter five will explain in fuller detail just *why* practice is so important in a Lamaze birth. Let it be sufficient to say here that practice is the very heart of the method. If you do not intend to practice together, the classes will benefit you very little. You will have more knowledge than you would have had otherwise, but the key to a comfortable labor and delivery does not lie in knowledge alone; it is found in readiness—a combination of knowledge and physical ability.

An athlete would not compete in the Olympics without years of training, priming, and skill-building. Fortunately, although having a baby is a physical event, it does not take years of preparation. It does, however, take several weeks of diligent work together to achieve a good degree of success. Here are some things you can do to gain the most from each practice session:

1. Use it as a time to unwind and communicate and the minutes will go by much faster.

2. Try not to wait until bedtime, when you are both tired. Early in the evening, after a relaxing meal and showers, seems to be a good time.

3. Assemble all of your "equipment" in advance—pillows, watch, this book. The mother should wear loose-fitting clothes and empty her bladder to make sure she is as comfortable as possible.

4. If you cannot practice together every day because of working schedules, school, or other problems, make a tape recording of one session. Then the mother can play it and practice even in the coach's absence.

5. The woman should not close her eyes, even when completely released. The only way a coach can be *sure* she is "awake and aware" is if her eyes are open. *Note*: If her eyes are darting around the room, she is not well released. She should stare at a "focal point"—an object in the room, her toes, or you. A clock with a second hand makes an excellent focal point because she can also regulate her breathing as she watches it.

6. The coach should check for muscular tension in the face, neck, and throat while she is breathing.

7. Intersperse the practice contractions with short periods of neuromuscular release to change the pace a little.

8. Occasionally she should "mess up" a contraction in some way—add tension somewhere or breathe at the wrong rate. This will give the coach expertise in detecting problems.

9. Some couples even like to "trade places" for an evening, allowing each to gain a new perspective on what the other is having to do!

10. It is important to practice right through interruptions, such as the ringing phone or doorbell. The contractions of real labor won't "wait."

11. If you become dizzy during a session, stop for a while and breathe slowly. As you become more proficient with your breathing, this will no longer occur. Women who have established cor-

rect breathing patterns through much practice seldom hyperventilate in labor.

12. Practice in every feasible position and location you might choose for labor. Be innovative!

13. Take a "cleansing breath" at the beginning and end of each contraction. This is simply a big, deep inhalation and expulsion of air—like a sigh. If you lose control or lose your rhythm during a contraction, simply take another cleansing breath and try again.

14. Make sure that you inhale and exhale equal amounts with each breath. When you do, it is possible to continue with one type of breathing almost indefinitely without growing tired.

REMEMBER, you do not have to perform "perfectly" during each practice session, but the mere act of practicing regularly will greatly increase your chances of doing things properly in labor.

WORKING TOGETHER

Daily Practice Sessions
1. Express Complementary Air—2 or 3 times per sitting, twice a day.
2. Butterfly—practice 5 times a day—bounce 5-10 times.
3. Pelvic Rock—three times a day, 20 "rocks" per session.
4. Kegel exercises—50-100 times a day.
5. Deep relaxation or conscious release—20 minutes a day.

Topics for Discussion and Action
1. What do you hope to gain from your childbirth classes?
2. Which time of day will be the best for the two of you to arrange to practice *together*?
3. COACH ONLY: Keep track of the mother's eating habits for one full day this week and help her to analyze how she "measures up."

CHAPTER 4

All About Labor

Fear not, for I am with you. Be not dismayed, for I am thy God. I will strengthen thee . . . I will help thee . . . I will uphold thee. (Isa. 41:10)

Get ready for the most exciting experience of your entire life! God has concentrated the whole essence of life into the birth experience. The entire range of emotions is experienced, and for many, the delivery is climaxed by a deep spiritual sensation.

Labor is the process of expelling the baby by contractions of the uterus. The average labor lasts 12-14 hours for a primipara, and 6-8 hours for a multipara. Labor is divided into three stages. *First Stage* occupies 90% of labor time. It includes *effacement* and *dilatation. Effacement* is the softening and thinning of the cervix, the neck of the uterus. This sometimes happens two to three weeks before labor actually begins, or may occur in early labor. *Dilatation* is the opening of the cervix. The doctor charts the progress of labor in terms of dilatation. It is measured in centimeters or fingers: ten centimeters or five fingers is full dilatation. (See chart on the next page.)

Dilatation can be slow until five centimeters is reached, and this takes about two-thirds of the total labor time. After five centimeters, the pace of the contractions speeds up and it takes only about one-third of the total labor time to complete dilatation.

Transition is the finale of First Stage. Dilatation goes from eight centimeters to ten, and takes only 10-60 minutes to complete. Check the labor chart in chapter five for the signs of transition.

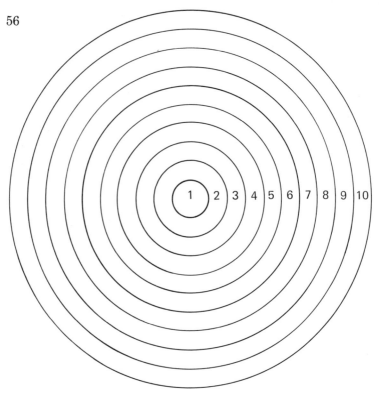

1 2 3 4 5 6 7 8 9 10

Cervical Dilatation Chart (in centimeters)

Second Stage is the delivery of the baby. It is the pushing stage and involves 10% of the total labor time. It can be as short as five minutes or as long as one-and-one-half hours. With proper pushing the sensations during this time are quite pleasant and provide an ecstatic climax for labor.

"Crowning" is when the widest part of the baby's head emerges. The mother feels the sensations of burning, tingling, and pins-and-needles. After this, "God's anesthesia" occurs, causing the perineum to become numb from the pressure of the baby's head.

Third Stage is the expulsion of the placenta. This generally occurs with one contraction 5-20 minutes after the birth. Most women forget that their work is not done, and need to be reminded to push again. Proper management of Third Stage is vital (especially with a home birth) for having a complication-free postpartum period.

Communicating with Your Doctor

Many couples feel that to have a good birth experience, they must fight tooth and nail with their doctor. This is certainly not necessary. The doctor wants you to have an enjoyable birth experience, but his main concern, and rightfully so, is the safety of you and your baby. The key word is *teamwork.* If there is any complication, the doctor will conduct the labor in the manner safest for mother and child. The nurse gives the doctor reports on the mother's condition and supplies the mother with helps for her comfort. The coach is mainly concerned with the mother's comfort. He gives her needed support and encouragement as well as guiding her through her birthing techniques. She notifies the coach of any changes in her condition and works under the supervision of the coach. Each member of the team has a vital part in the birth experience.

You may not desire some of your doctor's procedures for your own labor. This should be discussed openly and frankly with your doctor. If this is hard for you, write a letter. Letters can be an effective way of opening the lines of communication. The following are excerpts from a publication called *Pep Talk.* They include a letter written by an expectant mother to her doctor and the advice she offers others:

"First, let me say that I was impressed by you both, and I am very confident that you and the staff at the hospital will give me the finest medical care possible. But, I believe your concern for me as a patient extends, as well, to me as a person, since the two are inseparable. There are certain aspects of my delivery that matter very much to me, and I would appreciate all the attention and consideration you can give them.

"I have thought very carefully about the following requests I would like to make concerning my labor and delivery. Please note that these are requests, not demands, and that all of them are not special services I want but rather special services I do *not* want, if it is at all possible. . . . Believe me, I understand completely that everything I ask carries a certain amount of 'risk.' However, I feel these are areas where the likelihood of risk is small in my case. If the efforts to minimize risk means that I must sacrifice my own natural inclinations, needs, and preferences, then I think the price is too high. Nobody cares more about the health and safety of me and my baby than I do. If the smallest indication of trouble arises, I would welcome the intervention of any drugs, equipment, or procedures that you or the staff judge imperative. But unless a problem develops, please pay me the compliment of allowing me some expression in the birth of my baby. I wish to *give birth*, not to just be delivered."

After she had her baby, the mother had this advice to offer: "First, be *diplomatic* (you always have a better chance of succeeding); second, be *reasonable* (don't make outlandish requests, and be openminded to your doctor's point of view); third, and most important, be *informed*! Make sure you know what you're talking about so you don't make decisions on some flimsy evidence or some popular misconceptions."[1]

Alternatives to Routine Hospital Delivery

If you decide that you would like things done differently from the usual procedures, it is important that you plan ahead. Any and all requests should be discussed and resolved in advance with your doctor, nursing staff, and/or hospital. The suggestions on this page do not necessarily guarantee a perfect birth. They are merely guidelines from which you can plan your own unique birth experience.

In Labor. Ask that medication or inducing agents not be administered *routinely*.

Ask to have available during labor, juice (if allowed) or at least water and ice chips; request light food if labor is prolonged.

Request to have a partial "prep" (clipping of some perineal hair rather than shaving), or no prep at all.

The Birth. Request the option to use a different position, slant board, and/or no stirrups in delivery.

Ask that an episiotomy not be done *routinely*, but that the matter be decided as the baby's head crowns. (See section on episiotomy in chapter six.)

Ask for a spontaneous delivery of the placenta if possible, and that adequate time be allowed for the cord to stop pulsating before it is cut. (This allows the baby to receive all the blood that is rightfully his.)

Check to see if the hospital and doctor allow the father to cut the cord and bathe or clean the baby, or at least supervise these procedures.

Request that the mother's hands not be strapped down and that she be allowed to hold the baby immediately upon giving birth, to warm the baby with her own body rather than with an incubator.

After the Birth. Ask that the parents and baby not be separated *at all* after the birth, that there be little or no time spent in the recovery room, and that mother and baby be allowed to room together immediately.

Ask if alternatives to silver nitrate (for the baby's eyes) are permitted by law.

Request that the baby not be bathed immediately; the vernix may be rubbed into the skin as "nature's cold cream."

If the baby must be kept in the nursery, request that he not be fed water, sugar water, or formula, as these will decrease the mother's milk supply. Request breastfeeding "on demand."

Check to see if the hospital has an early discharge program, in which mother and baby can go home six to twelve hours after delivery if no problems are anticipated. Early examination of the baby by a pediatrician is usually essential for early discharge.

It is not necessary for the baby to be circumcised in the hospital, although it is convenient. Science has now learned what Bible scholars knew all along—it is better to wait until after the eighth day. The baby's blood clots better then, due to an increase in vitamin K production.

MAKE SURE THAT ALL EXCEPTIONS TO THE ROUTINE ARE IN WRITING!

BIRTH REPORT*

I am the mother of Aaron, who was delivered by the Pavlov-Lamaze method. I became interested in Lamaze classes after my sister had her baby by this method. She told me what a wonderful experience she and her husband had, so both Joe and I decided this was the only way to go!

---

*Used by permission of Charlene Ward.

A Typical Labor Room

Recovery/Postpartum Room

An Alternative Birth Center Room
(used for both labor and delivery)

The first indication that my labor was beginning was when I lost the mucus plug Thanksgiving morning. The rest of the day I felt as if I had indigestion. At about 8:00 p.m. my water broke; it was time to head for the hospital. On our way to the hospital, Joe and I timed my contractions. They were sporadic, ranging from six to ten minutes apart. I then began using my slow deep breathing, effleurage, and relaxation exercises.

At the hospital, the nurses checked me and found that I was dilated two centimeters. My doctor had said that he preferred that I be prepped, so as soon as I arrived in the labor room I was prepped, had my temperature taken, and was given an enema.

Between 9:30 and 11:30 I dilated from two to four centimeters, still using slow deep chest breathing and sometimes using a fast deep chest and panting, trying to find the most effective method. Effleurage was extremely effective throughout my entire labor. By 12:30 I was up to five centimeters.

Between five and seven centimeters, I became very sleepy. For a few minutes I found myself dozing; I awakened in the middle of a contraction—this really hurt and I was scared! My husband saw what was happening and gave me a real pep talk! After seeing what confidence he had in this method and in me, I had no trouble staying awake.

I was extremely nauseated because I had been eating all day. When I reached almost eight centimeters, they called my doctor and informed him of my nausea. He ordered a shot and was soon on his way to the hospital. I was leary of what was actually in the hypo, but the nurse assured me that all it would do was help the nausea.

The doctor arrived at 1:45 a.m., checked me, and found I was now at eight centimeters. By this time I was in transition and I felt a tremendous urge to push. The nurses wheeled me into the delivery room while Joe and the doctor were getting themselves ready. The doctor gave me an episiotomy. I pushed twice on each of the next three contractions and Aaron was born at 2:53 a.m. I'll always remember the look on my husband's face when our baby was born, and the tears of joy we both shed! Any couple who experiences its child's birth together is brought much closer together.

Practical Lesson 2

Labor Breathing. All labor breathing is done with the chest. This provides enough oxygen for the stress of contractions without causing undue pressure on the uterus.

Slow Deep Chest Breathing is used during early labor. Inhale a comfortable amount of air through your nose and exhale it through your mouth. Breathe in a slow, even pace, about 6-10 breaths a minute.

Fast Deep Chest Breathing is used when labor contractions become stronger. Speed chest breathing to 16-20 breaths a minute.

Accelerated-Decelerated Breathing is used when contractions become strong enough to be felt like waves (increasing in intensity, then decreasing). Start with slow deep chest breaths, increase, peak at a fast deep chest breath, then decrease.

The Cleansing Breath is done at the beginning and end of every contraction. It is simply one deep inhalation and exhalation.

Neuromuscular Release. Wear loose clothing and empty your bladder so you'll be comfortable. Lie in a semi-supine position.

"Contract" right arm. Release the tension.

"Contract" left arm. Release the tension.

"Contract" right leg. Release the tension.

"Contract" left leg. Release the tension.

When these limbs can be relaxed well, try your right arm and left leg and then your left arm and right leg. Learn to respond immediately to commands to release.

When a limb is contracted, mentally concentrate on keeping the rest of your body relaxed.

Kegel Step II. May be done on the toilet or other low chair or stool. Lean forward with knees apart, rest elbows on knees. Concentrate on contracting just the vagina and urethra. Release these and then try to contract just the anus. Repeat, contracting all three at once. Release.

WORKING TOGETHER

Daily Practice Sessions
The expectant mother should practice the following three times daily. At least one of these sessions should be done with the coach.

10-15 minutes neuromuscular release (this can be interspersed with the following contractions)

5 60-second contractions, slow deep chest

3 60-second contractions, fast deep chest

5 60-second contractions, accelerated-decelerated

Do throughout the day:

Expression of Complementary Air

Pelvic Rocks

Kegel Exercises (both kinds)

Butterflies

Analyze what muscles are involved in your daily chores. Release any muscles that aren't necessary for the task at hand.

Topics for Discussion and Action
1. *Coach*: During these last few weeks, arrange to accompany your wife on a prenatal visit. If you have not already done so, meet the doctor and discuss your feelings with him.
2. *Wife*: Attend the "maternity tea" if your hospital has one.
3. Discuss your plans for a Lamaze birth with your doctor.

CHAPTER 5

Now What Do I Do?

GUIDELINES FOR COACHES

And thou shalt have joy and gladness, and many shall rejoice at his birth. (Luke 1:14)

What Is the "Threshold of Sensation"? Your *threshold of sensation* is the level of intensity stimuli must reach before you become aware of them. An example of this would be that, although all the organs in your body are working when you are alert and in good health, you do not feel these organs functioning. Stimuli are constantly being sent from each organ; they travel along nerve pathways to the brain which receives information about the functions of the organs. But these stimuli, upon reaching the brain, are stopped. They meet a barrier they cannot cross because they are not strong enough. The stimuli are too weak to cross the brain's *threshold of sensation.*

Yet, at certain times you may feel your internal organs in an unpleasant, even painful sort of way. This may result from strong emotions such as shock, fear, anger, or anxiety. The brain's threshold of sensation is suddenly lowered, allowing these same stimuli to cross over the threshold. The threshold of sensation can also be raised. This can be done by concentrating on something important, such as the releasing and breathing techniques.

Pavlovian Conditioning. A Russian scientist, Ivan P. Pavlov, is actually responsible for the basis of the Lamaze method. Although Pavlov was not a Christian, we believe that God often reveals to men, through science, the ways in which His laws of nature can be understood and used for our benefit. In this case, Pavlov was the man who first defined "conditioned response"— the ability of the brain to *learn* to respond to a certain stimulus in a certain way. Most of us remember learning of Pavlov's experiments. He trained dogs to salivate at the ringing of a bell by first presenting them with food as the bell rang. After many times, he could ring the bell and offer *no* food, and the dogs would salivate anyway; for this had become a *learned* response to the bell-ringing. They had become conditioned.

Your practice sessions will condition you to respond correctly during labor. As you rehearse the neuromuscular release and breathing techniques together, with the coach using the terms "contraction begins" and "contraction ends," your brain will create a link between the beginning of a contraction and your learned reaction to it. Thus, during labor the actual contraction will trigger the learned response. If well learned, your response will be almost automatic and will greatly improve the sensations of labor.

Pavlov also found that if he discontinued the pairing of the sound and food, or if he was not consistent in pairing the food and sound each time, the dogs lost their conditioned response. In like manner, if you cut down or stop practicing altogether, you will lose your conditioning. That is why it is so important for you to practice every day, from now until the day you begin labor.

Though the ultimate responsibility for success lies with the mother, the coach's role in labor is extremely important. The coach must understand the emotional and physical stages the mother will go through during labor so that he can help her respond. The coach must be "conditioned" so well that he can readily and accurately adopt a course of action.

The coach and mother should carefully study the "Labor Chart" in this chapter and learn as much of it as possible. When labor actually starts, the coach should time the contractions and keep track on the "Coach's Record of Labor." He should also make sure that the "Information Checklist" is filled out.

LABOR CHART

WHAT IS HAPPENING	HOW IT FEELS	MOTHER'S ROLE	COACH'S ROLE
Changes in the last month			
Braxton-Hicks contractions.	Become far more noticeable, sometimes mistaken for labor.	Practice labor techniques with all prelabor contractions.	Time any contraction you see her breathe with, also check for release. Speak of contractions, not "pains."
Heavy mucus discharge.	Moist and sticky.	Bathe twice a day; wear mini pads.	Make her feel beautiful and loved.
Lightening—baby drops and the head is engaged into the pelvis.	Baby no longer does "flip-flops," you can breathe again, you feel a lot of pressure on your bladder.	Simplify life-style to provide peaceful surroundings.	Protect the mother from tense situations. Help with housework. Help the time go quickly.
Loss of water weight (3-4 days before labor)	Feel less swollen, joints stop aching.	Time is close! Be sure everything is ready and bags are packed.	Complete all last-minute details (have you toured the hospital, preregistered?).
Spurt of energy (1-2 days before labor)	Terrible urge to scrub floors and rearrange furniture.	Save your energy for labor.	Rest up—in a couple of nights you may not get to sleep at all.
Nature's enema.	Diarrhea, may be accompanied by cramps.	Do not take medication to control.	Reassure her that nothing is wrong; watch for other signs of labor (you may notice them before she does).

Signs of Beginning Labor

Dislodging of mucus plug (bloody show), can happen anytime from two weeks prior to labor to during labor.	Sticky mucus discharge, pinkish to dark red.	Wear mini pads; note the time on the information check list.	Make business arrangements so you will be able to leave on a moment's notice. Keep pillows, blanket and suitcase in car wherever you go.
Rupture of membranes (bag of waters)—usually happens in active labor, but can happen 24 hours prior to labor.	Does not hurt; you may feel a "pop" deep within; can gush or trickle. If during labor, it can change the characteristics of contractions.	Do not bathe, shower only. Call doctor. If baby's head is not engaged, keep your feet elevated.	Mop up, using old towels. Note the time and characteristics on the information checklist.
Contractions—if you aren't having them, you can't be in labor.	Pressure in back, pressure in pelvis, menstrual or gaslike cramps, tightness at lower sides, working around to front, or vice-versa.	Keep occupied with light activity. Check for real labor—if you've been working hard, rest; if you've been resting, move around a bit. False contractions will stop.	Note the time and characteristics on the information checklist. Help time and evaluate contractions. Remind her to empty her bladder every hour.

First Stage
(Dilatation of cervix)

Early Phase Effacement 0-100% May occur 2-4 weeks prior to labor.	Short, light contractions; 15-30 sec. long, 5-20 min. apart, often irregular.	Stay released; see "Contractions," above.	Encourage her that the contractions are doing some good. If she's hungry, fix her something light.

Dilatation: 0-4 cm.	Contractions 30-60 sec. long; 5-20 min. apart. May feel some peaks.	When needed use Lamaze techniques. See "Contractions."	Watch for signs of progress. See "Contractions."
Active Phase Dilatation: 4-8 cm.			
5 cm.	60 sec. contractions; reach strongest intensity. You become very flushed and have a short time of anxiety. Contractions 4 minutes apart.	Do not eat any solid food; your stomach has stopped functioning. Adapt to contractions, resting between them.	Prevent others from bothering her during contractions. Communicate her needs to the medical staff. Help her use the Lamaze technique, using effleurage, counter-pressure and touch release. During low points lift her morale.
6-8 cm.	Contractions 60-75 sec. long; 2-3 min. apart. Peaks may be longer; pressure during contractions. Takes much concentration.	Change positions every half hour. Work hard on release; may help to concentrate on uterine heat.	She's more inward, so you must work harder to find out what she needs or wants. Offer her a wet cloth to moisten her lips (ice chips if available).
Transition Dilatation: 8-10 cm.	Lasts 10-60 minutes. Contractions 60-90 secs. long, though not uncommon to be longer, and are 1-2 mins. apart. May seem like one long contraction with many peaks. May be accom-	Work with each contraction as it comes; stay alert. Use pant-blow with the urge to push.	She needs you most now; don't leave her. May need your help to overcome transition signs. Remind her that she is just about over the hard part. She may not want to be touched

			anymore; adapt your coaching to it. If it doesn't bother her, a firm massage of the thighs will relieve leg ache.
	panied by urge to push, extreme pressure, discouragement, irritability, vomiting, cold feet, sleepiness, shaking, loss of inhibitions and/or loss of time perception.		
Second Stage Expulsion Phase	Contractions 60 sec. long, 2-5 min. apart. You feel great—like you can run a mile. Can feel the baby descending thru the birth canal. "Crowning" burns for a minute then goes numb.	Push when you know you are fully dilated. Stop pushing when crowning. Remember to keep the rest of your body released.	Have a mirror handy so mother can watch. Remind her of steps to pushing if she forgets. Help her into position for pushing. Tell her to look in the mirror and see the birth.
Third Stage Birth of placenta (afterbirth)	5-20 min. after birth. Mild contractions often unnoticed. Generalized trembling common.	Usually takes only one push.	Stay close to her and baby—for bonding. Bask in the after-glow. May want to go with baby to supervise washing or participate in the early baby care as planned in cooperation with the doctor.

INFORMATION CHECKLIST

Husband's work phone _____

Name of birth attendant _____ Phone _____

Name of hospital _____ Phone _____

Name of baby's doctor _____ Phone _____

Name of childbirth instructor _____ Phone _____

Paramedics' phone _____
    (in case of emergency)

WHAT TO TELL THE DOCTOR:
    1. Contractions
        a. When did they start? _____
        b. How long do they last? _____
        c. How far apart are they? _____
        d. How strong are they? _____
    2. Mucus plug
        a. When was it dislodged? _____
        b. What did it look like? _____
    3. Bag of Waters
        a. When did it break? _____
        b. Did it gush or trickle? _____

COACH'S RECORD OF LABOR:

Contraction Begins	Ends	Length of Contractions	How Far Apart	Comments

Contraction Begins	Ends	Length of Contractions	How Far Apart	Comments

Contraction Begins	Ends	Length of Contractions	How Far Apart	Comments

WHAT TO DO WHEN . . .

	Mother	*Coach*
She hyperventilates (tingling, light-headedness, dizziness).	Slow down breathing. Breathe into paper bag or cupped hands. Concentrate on *release*.	Help her to regulate breathing by breathing *with* her; check for release.
She experiences back labor or has a backache during labor.	Try tailor-sitting, pelvic-rock position, side-lying, etc.	Help her change positions frequently; apply heat or cold; apply lots of counter-pressure and massage.
Labor is fast-moving.	Believe what you feel! Breathe as fast as you need to, but as slowly as possible to stay comfortable. Analyze and adapt with *every* contraction.	Be especially concerned with her release; place hand on her lower abdomen to detect oncoming contractions and warn her of them.

She becomes dis-couraged or feels the method isn't working.	Concentrate on each contraction as it comes—don't look into the past or future. Try one contraction *without* using techniques to prove their effec-tiveness to yourself.	Suspect transition. Call out 15-second intervals during contractions. Breathe *with* her. Use touch-release. Emphasize *any* change, no matter how small. Help her to stay released and comfortable *between* contrac-tions.
Her limbs are shaking.	Check for hyper-ventilation.	Massage—3 strokes on inner thigh (or arm) and one on outer, using the palm of your hand. Cover her with blankets.
The staff is uncoop-erative.	Shut them out mentally and rely solely on your coach for communication. Let him run inter-ference for you.	Take charge for your wife—she is *working*! Be asser-tive, but diplomat-ic—consider their point of view.

A FATHER'S BIRTH REPORT*

Around 5:30 a.m. I woke up and found myself alone in bed; I heard dishes rattling in the sink. I asked Joyce what was happening and she told me the contractions had started so she was trying to get the dishes done.

Joyce's pregnancy had worried me from the start; I had seen her suffer many attacks of bronchial asthma that left her weak and concentrating on nothing but the next breath of air. I often wondered what would happen to her under the stress of labor. I had attended the childbirth classes at first only because Joyce

---

*Used by permission of Ralph Milburn.

wanted me to, but soon I became fascinated by the birth process. The classes gave me a new outlook. However, the fact that the Lamaze method deals mostly with breathing techniques bothered me. I really didn't think my wife would be able to handle it. We began practicing every day and soon Joyce could perform all the levels of breathing, even the fast pant, for indefinite periods of time. On that final Tuesday she was put to the test, and for over 14 hours she breathed like a pro!

Throughout Joyce's labor the baby was in a posterior presentation (face up) so the progress of her labor did not follow the birth chart. The contractions were inconsistent, always less than 5 minutes apart, but varying widely in length and intensity. After six hours of labor she had only dilated one cm. From 5:30 a.m. to 7:00 p.m. the contractions continued to come one to five minutes apart.

I had expected everything to be a lot easier than it was, but Joyce really had to *work* to stay on top of the contractions. At 5:30 p.m. (6 cm.) they broke her water, and then things really began to happen. Transition began immediately and lasted 1½ hours. Joyce was sleepy and irritable, and I began to feel a little helpless! However, she never stopped her panting, never lost control, never moaned or groaned, and had no desire for medication. At 6:50 they offered medication, reminding her that if she did not take it then, it would not take effect before the birth. She refused, realizing that the hardest part was over. I was then told to put on my gown and wait to be called to the delivery room.

When I entered the delivery room, Joyce was pushing. I sat at her head and talked to her. Soon I could see the head crowning, and the episiotomy was made. In a few minutes the head was out and then came the whole baby, purple and screaming. At 7:22 p.m., I was the proud father of an eight-pound five-ounce boy!

As the cord was clamped and cut, Joyce got to hold our son briefly before he was taken away. In the recovery room she looked tired, relieved and satisfied—all in one. She had accomplished her goal—to be alert during the birth of her baby. And I had been a participant in that birth. Every father should be able to help his wife with her labor. He will experience a new sense of joy and gain new respect for his wife.

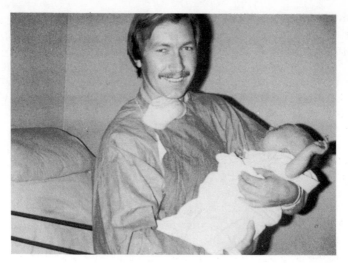

Practical Lesson 3

Effleurage. This is a light, fingertip massage of the abdomen. It helps to release the abdominal muscles and provides another point of concentration, increasing the threshold of sensation. Practice effleurage with all types of breathing.

Neuromuscular Release. Continue to work with the limb combinations that you have already learned, and add more difficult combinations. Throughout each day think about how your muscles feel. Which muscles are tense? Is there more tension than necessary for your activity? If so, try to release the excess tension.

Breathing. PANTING is done through the mouth, exclusively, because of the speed at which you will be breathing during contractions as labor advances. Dryness of the mouth and throat often accompanies mouth breathing. It is helpful to place the tongue behind the upper teeth, thus deflecting the air and moistening it as it enters your mouth.

As you try a practice contraction using fast deep chest breathing, begin inhaling as well as exhaling *through your mouth* at some point during the contraction. Now you are panting.

SLOW PANT is a shallow, more rapid type of breathing, to be used as labor progresses. It is done entirely through the mouth and at approximately 60 breaths per minute—or one per second.

MEDIUM PANT is more rapid—shallow and superficial—approximately 90 breaths per minute.

Kegel Step III. Sit on the floor or bed with your legs out in front of you. Contract the pelvic floor strongly, holding as long as possible. While holding the pelvic floor tension, cross your ankles slowly and uncross them. Release.

WORKING TOGETHER

Daily Practice Sessions

Practice one of the following with your coach, twice a day:

    10 minutes neuromuscular release

    Do effleurage with all breathing:

    3 60-second contractions, slow deep chest

    2 60-second contractions, accelerate from slow deep chest to fast deep chest, decelerate

    1 60-second contraction, fast deep chest with switch-to-mouth

    4 30-second contractions, slow pant

    4 60-second contractions, accelerate from slow to medium pant, decelerate

    5 60-second contractions, accelerate from fast deep chest to medium pant, decelerate.

Continue with all other exercises.

Topics for Discussion and Action

1. *Wife*: After each practice session with your coach, switch roles and do the touch-release technique for your coach; then he can feel for himself the relaxation it brings!

2. Discuss: Is the father's role as "coach" completed in the delivery room, or is it only starting? What kind of support would a new mother need in the months to come?

CHAPTER 6

Well, At Least I'm Unique!

"Shall I bring to the point of birth and not give delivery?"
says the Lord. (Isa. 66:9, NASB)

The labor chart in chapter three represents the "average" labor. There are many births that do not follow this chart—most of these are not abnormal, just less common than "average" labor. Such variations are usually caused by a too-narrow *passage*, the baby's *position*, uterine *power*, or a combination of these.

Three types of dysfunctional uterine activity (power) can cause an "out of the ordinary" labor. They are *hypotonic* and *hypertonic* contractions, and *incoordinate* uterine activity. Hypotonic contractions are very mild and do not cause much actual labor progress. Hypertonic contractions are not effective either, but are quite powerful and hard to deal with. By all outward appearances, incoordinate uterine activity seems the same as hypertonic contractions. Physiologically, though, the two are caused by different factors.

Any or all phases of labor may detour from the birth chart:

A prolonged latent phase lasts over 20 hours for a primipara, or 13½ hours for a multipara. It's caused by breech presentation, a too small pelvis, premature breaking of the bag of waters or excessive analgesia.

A prolonged active phase usually occurs when the baby's head doesn't descend into the pelvis as expected. A too small pelvis or breech presentation can also cause a labor slowdown.

Secondary arrest is when the progress of labor stops altogether during active stages. It is often associated with maternal exhaustion, but can also be caused by a too small pelvis, too much medication or anxiety caused by being in a hospital.

Precipitate labors are extremely fast-moving labors. A primipara can dilate five centimeters in an hour. A multipara can reach full dilatation within an hour.

Posterior labors are far more common than they would appear to be, since most babies will change position before the actual birth. Dilatation may not progress at the average rate because the contractions are turning the baby. Medication will not make the baby turn faster; in fact, it could have an opposite effect. *Back labor* is very common with posteriors. Back labor differs from "backache" in that all sensations of contractions are inhibited by the stronger sensations in the back. If back labor occurs during your labor, get into a position that will take the weight of the baby off your back—side position, knee-chest, tailor-sitting, and pelvic-rock positions are all good. Have the coach apply counterpressure—the coach presses hard against your lower back with his hands, feet, or a hard object such as a rolling pin. Hot or cold compresses may help also.

Breech births may cause labors that are slow in first stage, but remarkably speeded up in second stage. Three to four percent of all births are breech. The contractions are often felt differently; they may feel like a pulling in the cervix, with possible discomfort in the thighs and lower back.

The doctor will x-ray the pelvic area to determine whether the head can pass through safely. (The head has no opportunity to mold, so a larger pelvic diameter is required.) A caesarean section will be performed if the results of the x-ray warrant it. If the birth is allowed to proceed vaginally, an episiotomy might be performed or forceps employed to aid in the delivery.

If you know before labor that the baby is in a breech position, try the pelvic-rock, knee-chest position or "tilt" exercise (illustrated on page 79) to turn the baby. The tilt posture involves lying on a firm surface, with the pelvis raised by pillows to a level of 9 to 12 inches above the head. This should be done twice a day for ten minutes at a time—on an empty stomach. It should be done from the time you discover the baby is breech until you learn that it has turned.

The "tilt" exercise

Another method of turning the baby is sometimes attempted by the doctor. He does this by grasping the baby through the mother's abdominal wall and turning the baby 180 degrees. This is not usually very successful, and carries some risk for the fetus.

Fetal monitoring provides a continuous, visible record of the infant's heart activity, while also measuring the frequency, duration, and strength of uterine contractions. There are two methods of fetal monitoring. The first is *indirect* or *external* monitoring, which consists of two units connected to a sensing device, held against the mother's abdomen by elastic belts. One of these units senses the infant's heartbeat, and the other senses the uterine contractions. The information then travels to the fetal monitoring machine which records it on a moving paper tape.

The second method of monitoring is called *direct* or *internal* monitoring. A small electrode is passed through the birth canal and attached to the baby's scalp to record heart activity. Another device, a small, soft plastic catheter, can also be inserted into the uterine cavity to measure contractions. The membranes must be broken and cervix dilated before internal monitoring can be used. This is more accurate than external monitoring and allows the mother more freedom of movement.

Advantages of using fetal monitor:

1. Fetal problems can be detected during labor, supposedly reducing the stillbirth rate.

2. Contractions can be detected before they are felt by the mother. This insures that she stays one step ahead of the contractions.

Advantages of NOT using fetal monitor:

1. External monitoring is very confining, and some Lamaze techniques, such as effleurage and frequent position changing, are more easily performed without it.

2. You may assume positions other than the supine position (flat on your back), which is customary for external monitoring, but also notorious for causing fetal distress.

3. Some studies have shown that fetal monitors have not changed the stillbirth rate, but have caused an enormous increase in the caesarean section rate.

4. There is no risk of infection to the baby.

5. It is not necessary to artificially rupture the membranes, as it would be with internal monitoring.

6. Labor will be more personalized, as the coach and staff will be paying attention to the laboring mother and not the monitor.

NOTE: HIGH-RISK MOTHERS AND MOTHERS WITH LABOR COMPLICATIONS SHOULD BE MONITORED!!

THE EPISIOTOMY

In recent years the episiotomy (an incision to enlarge the perineum at the time of birth) has become an almost routine procedure. Researchers indicate that in America about 70% of the women giving birth have an episiotomy. The question is not whether the episiotomy is a valuable surgical procedure, but whether or not its *routine* performance is valuable to *you* as an individual. There are several situations in which an episiotomy is desirable because of certain physical factors. In a case of fetal distress it can help the baby to be born more quickly. It can prevent a premature baby's head from battering against the perineum for prolonged periods of time. It is also very useful in the case of a forceps delivery, breech delivery, delayed delivery due to tissue which will not stretch enough, and in the presence of heart trouble in the mother whose bearing-down effort needs to be reduced.

The main advantages given for routine performance of episiotomies are twofold, and questionable:

1. It helps to prevent a jagged tearing of the perineum, which is more difficult to repair and takes longer to heal than a straight incision.
2. It will supposedly help the pelvic floor muscles resume their original shape, tone, and function, although no research has borne this out except in the case of forceps deliveries.

If your baby's birth does not fall into one of the "difficult" categories mentioned previously, you have reason to question the benefits of the procedure. Many people feel that the reasons for avoidance are worth a second look:

1. There are other ways to prevent tearing of the perineum, as we shall discuss shortly.
2. Consistent use of the Kegel exercises after delivery (contracting and releasing the pelvic floor repeatedly) will help more than an episiotomy in restoring the pelvic floor muscles and tissue to proper shape and function.
3. Midline episiotomies are notorious for extending, by tearing, all the way to the anal sphincter (rectum) and requiring additional repair work.
4. About 6% of women who have had an episiotomy feel discomfort during intercourse for weeks or months following the birth.
5. The stitches to repair the incision after delivery must be made at a critical time in the parent-child relationship, when bonding could be taking place. In spite of local anesthesia, they are usually felt somewhat and can interfere with the mother's interest in her baby.
6. Recovery from the stitches also occurs at a critical time in the life of the mother, and excessive pain or discomfort can even cause postpartum depression and lactation failure.

Although the United States has an episiotomy rate of at least

70%, many nations have lower rates. In Australia it is about 30%; in England 15%; and in the Netherlands, estimates are as low as 6-8%.[2] In France the rate is 33% for primiparas, and only 5% for multiparas among the patients of Dr. Pierre Vellay, one of our consultants. In light of the apparent fact that episiotomies are not necessary much of the time, you may wish to discuss with your doctor the possibility of avoiding one. Various procedures can be followed, instead, to help the perineum remain intact. Arrive at an understanding *beforehand* with your doctor as to which he would allow:

1. A position other than the lithotomy position (lying flat on your back with legs in stirrups) will allow your body to work with gravity. Squatting is very good (or side-lying, in the case of a baby that is descending rapidly).

2. Application of counterpressure to the perineum to allow it time to stretch *slowly* is often effective.

3. Application of warm compresses during the pushing stage will ease perineal tension.

4. Conscious release of the pelvic floor is *essential* to avoiding an episiotomy.

Rebecca Rowe Parfitt states that the three critical factors in the avoidance of an episiotomy are: (1) TIME—You and the doctor must take the time to let the perineum stretch fully, and delay the final, gentle pushing until the opening is big enough for the baby to fit through; (2) TEAMWORK—You and the doctor should prepare yourselves to try together for a nonepisiotomy delivery; (3) SKILL—The attendant must have expertise in knowing how to avoid the cut.[3]

If it does become necessary for you to have an episiotomy, there are two major types. The *median*, or *midline*, episiotomy carries the risk of extension to the anal sphincter, but it is easier to repair and bleeds less. The *mediolateral* cut is harder on the woman, and many experts feel that it provides no additional room for the baby.

If you have an episiotomy, care for it properly to insure the most rapid healing possible. Use a heat lamp twice daily for comfort, and take frequent Sitz baths. Your doctor can also recommend a local anesthetic spray if the discomfort is too great. It is better to sit on firm surfaces while healing is taking place, as it will require less effort to get back up. Kegel exercises should be done regularly and frequently.

Kegel exercises seem to be one of the greatest contributing factors to the healing of the perineal region, whether an episiotomy has been performed or not. Contracting and releasing the pelvic floor will improve circulation to the area and speed up the healing process. It will also help to restore tone, strength, and feeling to the muscles of the pelvic floor and perineal area, which have been stretched by the birth. They are important to *every* woman after delivery, whether she has had an episiotomy or not.

CAESAREAN BIRTHS

Today, 12-15% of all babies born in the United States are delivered by caesarean section. The caesarean rate exceeds 25% in some medical centers. With this in mind, every expectant couple should prepare themselves for the possibility that their labor might end with a caesarean.

A caesarean section is an incision made in the mother's abdomen to remove the baby. There are two types of incisions used today: the classical caesarean section and the lower segment caesarean section, often referred to as the "bikini cut." The classical caesarean section has in general been superseded by the lower segment procedure. Now, it is mainly used when the "bikini cut" is not medically feasible. The classical incision runs vertically from the navel down to the pubis. The lower segment incision runs horizontally across the cervix. The scar cannot be seen once the pubic hair grows out. With this incision there is a greater chance that subsequent pregnancies could end in spontaneous vaginal birth.

A caesarean section may be necessary for various reasons:

1. *The labor fails to progress satisfactorily.* This could occur if the baby's head is too large for the mother's pelvis (cephalopelvic disproportion), or if the mother's pelvis is tilted in such a way that the normal descent of the baby is prevented. Sometimes the cervix just will not dilate. Other times contractions slow down or stop all together.

2. *The baby is in the wrong position (transverse, breech,*

etc.). Babies often *can* be born safely in breech position, but doctors are becoming more reluctant to perform difficult deliveries. With some presentations the baby cannot be delivered except by caesarean.

3. *Problems can arise with the placenta and umbilical cord.* Sometimes the placenta separates from the uterine wall (abruptio placentae). In other cases the placenta covers the cervix (placenta previa), or the umbilical cord falls into the birth canal (prolapsed cord). All these problems cut off the oxygen to the baby.

4. *Labor is hazardous for women with diabetes or severe high blood pressure.* High blood pressure, along with toxemia, may not require a caesarean unless the blood pressure continues to rise during labor.

5. *The baby is in distress.* If during labor, the baby demonstrates a lack of oxygen by a lowered heart rate, and if this rate cannot be increased by a change of position and a greater intake of oxygen by the mother, a caesarean might be necessary. Over the past decade, the incidence of emergency caesareans has almost doubled. Fetal monitors have played an important part in this increase.

6. *The woman has had a previous caesarean.* A growing number of doctors are allowing women who have had previous caesareans to deliver subsequent babies vaginally. Most doctors, however, still believe, "once a caesarean—always a caesarean."

If the decision is made, that a caesarean section is needed, the coach is ushered out of the labor room. The mother's abdomen is washed and shaved from just below the breasts to the rectum, then painted with antiseptic. She is then draped with sterile sheets and adminstered anesthesia. A urinary catheter is inserted and an intravenous drip started.

In the delivery room the mother's arms are secured at right angles to her body and a screen is placed in front of her face to maintain a sterile field. Although the baby is delivered within 5 to 10 minutes, the mother remains in the delivery room another 40 minutes for the closing of the incision.

In itself, a caesarean section is an impersonal surgical procedure. With proper planning and support from the doctor, this procedure can provide a very rewarding, meaningful birth. Below are some suggestions that may make the caesarean birth a more positive experience. You may ask:

1. That the father be allowed to remain with the mother for the birth and recovery.

2. To have a "bikini cut" if medically feasible.

3. That the mother be allowed the choice of remaining awake (local anesthetic) or being asleep during the operation.

4. That the mother be allowed to hold and breastfeed the baby an adequate amount of time for bonding (the father should be allowed to hold the baby, too).

5. To have rooming-in (It's important, though, to have someone help with the baby care).

6. That the baby not be placed in the special care nursery routinely. The mother should be allowed to visit if he is placed in the special care nursery.

7. That the mother be allowed to wear beltless sanitary napkins.

8. That the mother be placed in a room with another woman who has had a caesarean birth.

9. That the mother be allowed to see her other children during her hospital stay. (This is very important since the caesarean mother must stay so much longer than the mother who delivers naturally.)

There are several organizations that have chapters across the country which are geared to helping the "caesarean couple." If you are expecting a caesarean birth or are having trouble adjusting to a caesarean you have already had, contact your childbirth instructor for the name and phone number of a group in your area.

Practical Lesson 4

Fast Pant. The fast pant is a very shallow, rapid form of breathing. The speed is approximately 120 breaths per minute, or two breaths per second. You may find it helpful to say "he" or "ha" with each exhalation—this will keep your panting shallow.

Pant-Blow. The pant-blow consists of a medium pant and a short, powerful exhalation with puffed cheeks, through pursed lips. After anywhere from one to five pants (you determine the rate), blow once, then repeat the pattern.

The purpose of the pant-blow is twofold. First, it provides a change in concentration. This makes it a "step up" from the fast pant. Second, it counteracts the urge to push. (Remember: the urge to push is a sign of transition, and usually comes before the cervix is completely dilated. Pushing at the first urge can cause pain and damage.) The urge to push can be *very* strong; the diaphragm will involuntarily push downward on the uterus unless it is being jerked up as a result of pant-blow breathing.

WORKING TOGETHER

Daily Practice Sessions

Practice twice daily, once with coach.

   10-15 minutes of neuromuscular release—concentrate on body awareness throughout the day.

Practice breathing in all positions, with effleurage:

   3 60-second contractions: accelerate slow deep chest to fast deep chest, then decelerate.

   3 60-second contractions: accelerate fast deep chest to slow pant, decelerate.

   3 60-second contractions: accelerate slow deep chest to medium pant for 30-second peak, then decelerate.

   3 60-second contractions: accelerate slow pant to fast pant for 20-second peak, decelerate.

   3 60-second contractions: pant-blow, blowing once for every one-to-five pants; find the rate most comfortable for you.

   2 15-second contractions; blow, no panting involved.

Continue daily exercises as before.

Topics for Discussion and Action

1. Discuss how you might react if faced with a non-conforming labor.
2. Discuss how you might feel if you were told a caesarean birth would be necessary.
3. Discuss what you think your partner's feelings would be after such a birth. Your own?

CHAPTER 7

"Does It Hurt Yet?" *

But refuse . . . old wives' fables. (1 Tim. 4:7)

Helen Wessel, author of *The Joy of Natural Childbirth*, has made the following observations on the subject of pain:

Our bodies have the remarkable ability to signal us when something is out of harmony with nature by causing us to "hurt." In this way, we are prompted to take steps to discover what is amiss and eliminate the *cause* of pain. An example of this would be when we withdraw our hand quickly from a pan of water that is too hot. The body signals the brain that it is not safe or natural for the hand to be exposed to such heat, and the brain responds appropriately.

Pain found in childbirth can be related to any of three basic causes. The first is *physiological*—actual mechanical reasons why labor is uncomfortable for a particular woman. Physiological causes may be disproportion, malpresentation, toxemia or other disease, general poor health, fatigue, laceration of tissues, or other unnatural conditions.

Another cause of pain in labor is *functional.* Functional causes are muscular tension and improper breathing, both of which are usually the result of negative emotions and fear. Muscular tension causes pain in many areas surrounding the uterus by inhibiting the birth process. Improper breathing by an anxious woman creates poor oxygenation of all muscles, especially the uterus, which requires so much oxygen to function properly. If there is a lack of oxygen to the working uterus, toxicity occurs and pain is the result.

---

*Condensed from a major address given by Helen Wessel at several childbirth conventions, and included in her new book *God's Design: The Christian Home* (Fresno: Bookmates, Int., 1981). Reprinted by permission.

The most common cause of pain in childbirth is the third, *emotional anxiety*. When a woman is ignorant of the birth process and fearful of what will happen next, the stage has been set for every physical sensation, no matter how small, to be interpreted as painful. It is important to remember that many "feelings" occur in labor, but that often that is all they are—sensations, not pain. Some of the things you might feel in labor are the movements of the uterus as it contracts, pressure as the baby descends through the birth canal, and the stretching of the tissues at the perineum as the birth draws near.

Mrs. Wessel offers several suggestions for the prevention of pain in childbirth:

1. Education concerning what is happening to one's body relieves anxiety and helps a woman to interpret physical sensations correctly.

2. The principles of good health must be faithfully applied, to be in optimum physical health for the birth.

3. Learning control of muscular relaxation must be faithfully practiced, so that one can release tension at will under any condition of stress.

4. Correct breathing for daily use, and helpful breathing techniques for comfort in labor should be learned in advance.

5. If pain still occurs, the staff should be alert to the possibility of a physiological problem which needs prompt medical attention, before resorting to medication.

MEDICATION

DRUG	DOSE	DURATION	MATERNAL SIDE EFFECTS	BABY SIDE EFFECTS
Analgesics: Drugs which relieve pain without necessarily inducing sleep (used during First Stage).				
Demerol or Mepergan	50-150 mg. 25 mg.	2-3 hrs. 2-3 hrs.	Slows down activity of the brain. May produce low blood pressure, euphoria, dizziness, dry mouth, respiratory depression, nausea, and sleepiness.	Respiratory depression. Behavioral responses may be altered up to 30 days, body heat loss, interference with neurological functioning.
Talwin	40-60 mg.	1½-2 hrs.	Respiratory depression, sedation, dizziness, nausea, low blood pressure, dry mouth, urinary retention. Compared to Demerol, the side effects are less intense.	Respiratory depression. More information not available.
Nisentil	30-60 mg.	1½-2 hrs.	Euphoria, sedation, dizziness, itching, sweating, depression, and nausea.	Respiratory depression.
Hypnotics: Do not affect the sensation of pain but lead to depression of the sensory functions of the brain and reflex activity of the spinal cord.				
Barbiturates: usually compounded with analgesics.				
Amytal Butisol Nembutal Luminal Seconal	30-50 mg. 15-30 mg. to 100 mg. 15-30 mg. to 100 mg.	7-8 hrs. 7-8 hrs. 4-6 hrs. 12-14 hrs. 4-6 hrs.	Reduce anxiety and tension. May cause low blood pressure, low pulse rate, disorientation, depressed responses—unable to deal with contractions, hangover.	Drug accumulates in fetal tissues. Possible poor Apgar score, low blood pressure, respiratory depression, poor muscle tone, decreased responsiveness and poor sucking.
Noctec Somnas	500 mg.-1 g.		May stop contractions.	Depression.
Tranquilizers: Relieve anxiety and promote calmness without inducing sleep or lessening pain.				

Drug	Dosage	Maternal effects	Fetal/newborn effects
Atarax, Vistaril (used with other medication to prevent nausea)	75-100 mg. 2-3 hrs.	May cause drowsiness, dry mouth, nausea. Relieves apprehension.	Unknown.
Valium	15-20 mg. IM* 2-3 hrs. 5-15 mg. IV* 1-1½ hrs.	Drowsiness, confusion, low blood pressure, urinary retention.	Fetal heart tones lose beat-to-beat variation, poor muscle tone, body heat loss, decreased attentiveness, slow adaptation to feeding, jaundice, and chromosome damage.
Librium	50-100 mg. IM, then 25-50 mg. as necessary	Same as Valium.	Same as Valium.
Equanil, Miltown	200-400 mg.	Drowsiness, dizziness, nausea, skin tingling, increased heart rate, and low blood pressure.	Less attentiveness, slow adaptation to feeding.
Phenothiazines Thorazine 25-50 mg. 6-8 hrs. Compazine 5-10 mg. 3-4 hrs. Sparine 25-50 mg. 3-4 hrs.		Low blood pressure, disorientation, lower convulsive threshold, increased heart rate or very slow heart rate, and drowsiness.	Depression, altered ability to maintain body temperature, diminished amount of oxygen in the blood, jaundice, poor muscle tone, and restlessness.

*IM—Intramuscular; *IV—Intravenous

| Phenergan | 25-50 mg. | 6-8 hrs. | Prevents and controls nausea and vomiting. Drowsiness, dizziness, CNS depression, dry mouth, confusion, low blood pressure, difficulty in keeping control, loss of inhibitions. | Unknown. Effects are difficult to pinpoint since drugs are often compounded with others. |
| Largon | 10-20 mg. | 3 hrs. | Dry mouth, increased blood pressure, low blood pressure (rarely). Similar to Phenergan. | Unknown. No depression observed. |

ANESTHESIA: Completely blocks pain impulses, resulting in a loss of feeling or sensation. May be administered locally, regionally, or generally.

REGIONALS AND LOCALS

Novocain	*Baby Side Effects*
Nesacaine	Found in low levels in baby's bloodstream. Most is metabolized fairly early.
Metycaine	
Blockain	
Pontocaine	

Lidocaine	*Baby Side Effects*
Marcaine	Increased or decreased heart rate, depression, convulsions.
Nupercaine	
Carbocaine	
Citanest	

Maternal Side Effects: Cardiac depression, decreased heart rate or increased heart rate, CNS depression, drowsiness, restlessness, dizziness, anxiety, and convulsions.

ADMINISTRATION

Paracervical Block: Blocks uterine pain. Given from 3 cm. to complete dilation. Used in conjunction with pudendal or saddle block.

Labor Side Effects	*Maternal Side Effects*	*Baby Side Effects*
Reduces the cervical stretching sensation, depression of contractions.	As listed above.	Decreased heart rate. Most severe depression occurs with pre-existing fetal distress, hyperactivity.

Pudendal Block: Analgesia in perineum for delivery and repair. Given after 10 cm., or after delivery for repair only.

Labor Side Effects	*Maternal Side Effects*	*Baby Side Effects*
Loss of bearing down reflex. Can lengthen second stage if given too early.	None if properly administered.	None, except with pre-existent fetal distress.

Saddle Block: Provides perineal anesthesia for forceps delivery and repair only. Given in second stage just before birth.

Labor Side Effects	*Maternal Side Effects*	*Baby Side Effects*
Usually will not arrest contractions. Urge to push is lost, forceps needed.	Lowered blood pressure, spinal headache, and weak bladder.	Sustained decrease in blood pressure, resulting in fetal depression.

Spinal block: Provides relief of pain from uterine contractions and in the perineal area for forceps delivery and repair. Results in total loss of feeling.

Labor Side Effects	*Maternal Side Effects*	*Baby Side Effects*
Same as for Saddle Block.	Same as for Saddle Block.	Same as for Saddle Block.

Caudal Block: Technically more difficult to administer. Given after 5 cm. through birth and repair.

Labor Side Effects	*Maternal Side Effects*	*Baby Side Effects*
May prolong labor, depression of contractions. May cause loss of bearing down reflex, with need for forceps.	Raised or lowered blood pressure, hypoventilation, diminished oxygen in the bloodstream.	Fetal distress, subtle changes, behavior alterations, poor muscle tone. May benefit "premie", through decreased forces during

Lumbar Epidural: Complete pain relief for uterine contractions, birth, and repair. Given at 6-7 cm. and is continuous.

Labor Side Effects
Decreased uterine contractibility, loss of bearing-down reflex, with need for forceps.

Maternal Side Effects
Less than those of Caudal: lowered blood pressure, depression, irritation of membranes.

Baby Side Effects
Body heat loss, trauma, delayed respiration, neurological problems.

Perineal Local: Numbness for repair and episiotomy only. Given just before episiotomy or just after the birth.

Labor Side Effects
None.

Maternal Side Effects
More uncomfortable repair if not used in combination with Block.

Baby Side Effects
Unknown.

GENERAL ANESTHESIA: Leads to total loss of consciousness (second stage).

Trimethylene
Ether
Nitrous Oxide
Trilene

The effects of these agents are difficult to evaluate because they are almost always used in combination with analgesics. Overall, the depressant effects are associated with circulatory and respiratory side effects which affect the function of the whole organism. May produce cardiac and respiratory depression, low blood pressure, depressed liver and kidney function, and skeletal muscle weakness for both mother and child.

Keep in mind that "side effects" occur with varying frequency, not all the time.

A MOTHER'S BIRTH REPORT*

When I became pregnant, I decided to have an unmedicated labor. I also wanted my husband to be as involved as possible. When my girlfriend told me about Lamaze classes, they seemed to be the ideal way of getting my husband involved. We both enjoyed the classes and learned so much.

As I approached my due date, an aunt sat me down and lectured me on how terrible labor was. She scared me out of my wits; I began to doubt that Lamaze would really help. That week I attended the final Lamaze class—all the woman had delivered except me. Hearing about how well they had done restored my confidence.

The following Friday, I woke up to discover that I had lost my mucus plug. Around 3:00 in the afternoon my bag of waters started trickling. Bruce and I went to the hospital at 6:00 that evening. I was checked and prepped. By then I had dilated to two centimeters.

My labor hadn't begun yet, but I was not allowed out of bed because the bag of waters had broken. Six hours later there was still no change—we were bored.

My doctor was concerned about infection, but decided to wait a couple of hours before he induced labor. As soon as he left the room, I felt something pop inside me. Immediately I had nature's enema, a great deal of pressure, and very strong contractions lasting 75 seconds and about 4 minutes apart. I panicked and hyperventilated. Bruce helped me to slow my panting down and instructed me to breathe into a paper bag. My limbs shook uncontrollably. Concentration on release and massage reduced the shaking, but we had to battle with the problem throughout the rest of the labor.

I was examined again at 1:30 a.m. I couldn't believe I was only 4 centimeters dilated. Contractions were lasting 90-120 seconds, with several peaks. I was almost ready to give up. My husband kept saying, "Let's just try one more contraction."

Finally, I was just too uncomfortable panting, so my husband told the nurse; the doctor came running. I was nine centimeters

*Used by permission.

so they wheeled me to the delivery room. Bruce and I blew through two contractions before the doctor told me I should have been pushing. I still didn't have an urge to push, and was very weak. I pushed once lightly to make sure it didn't hurt. The doctor didn't think I would be able to do it. Transition hadn't completely worn off yet, so I had to blow through another two contractions while the doctor gave me an episiotomy. Finally all the transition signs passed and I felt the urge to push. This time when I pushed I had all my strength—it felt so good! My husband kept saying, "Go! Go! Go! You're doing it! Keep going!" I must have held my breath for record time.

Then Bruce told me to look in the mirror and I saw Sarah being born. It was the most exciting thing that ever happened to me. Finally I was wheeled to the recovery room. My doctor brought Sarah to me to nurse after I stopped shaking. My husband and I have rarely felt so close as we did after experiencing our daughter's birth together.

Practical Lesson 5

Simulated Contractions. Now is the time to see if all that practice is working. To simulate a contraction, the coach will pinch on your shoulder, behind your knee or behind your ankle. As the contraction gets stronger, then peaks, so will the pinch. As the contraction tapers off, so will the force of the pinch. Start with a slow deep chest then adapt your breathing according to the pressure you feel.

Pushing. When you can finally start pushing, you will feel a great deal of relief—that is, if you are pushing properly. The most important thing is to keep the pelvic floor and legs completely released.

In a home birth you can experiment with different positions such as side position or squatting. But, in a hospital birth, the semi-supine position is best.

Pushing contractions build up to a peak very slowly, so take two deep cleansing breaths before pushing.

Instructions for pushing:
1. Take two deep cleansing breaths.

2. Take a third breath and hold for 10-15 seconds.
3. At the same time:
   Place hands under knees; pull legs up, spreading wide; keep elbows out; tuck in chin.
4. When you need more air, exhale while tipping your head back. Inhale quickly through your mouth; hold for another 10-15 seconds, with chin tucked in.
5. After the contraction lie back and rest.

During crowning the baby needs to descend very slowly so that the perineum will stretch rather than tear. When you feel the sensations of crowning, or are instructed by your doctor, stop pushing. A pant or pant-blow will give you good control.

To practice pushing with stirrups, lie on the floor with your legs spread wide on a chair. Pull yourself up by the chair legs; push as before.

Kegel Step IV. Your pelvic floor experiences three levels of tension. Total release of all the muscles is the first level. This is the state we want to achieve during the expulsion stage of labor. The second level is the one we should tighten to before coughing, sneezing, or straining, and when we consciously tighten them while standing or walking. The third level is one of extreme tension, used only briefly when "practicing." Practice moving smoothly from one level to another.

WORKING TOGETHER

Daily Practice Sessions
Practice twice daily, once with coach. Practice in all positions and with effleurage:

    15 minutes of neuromuscular release, interspersed with breathing. Practice all parts of the body. Make it difficult!

    2 60-second contractions—accelerate from slow deep chest to slow pant, 15-second peak, decelerate.

    2 60-second contractions—accelerate from slow pant to medium pant, 20-second peak, decelerate.

    4 90-second contractions—accelerate from slow pant to fast pant, 30-second peak, decelerate.

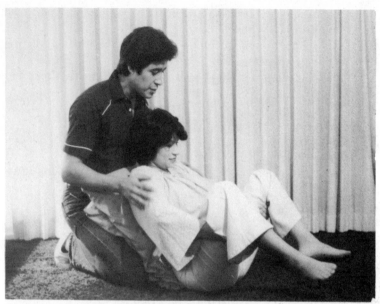

Proper Labor Room Pushing

Proper Delivery Room Pushing

2 60-second contractions—pant-blow, choosing your own rhythm.

2 60-second contractions—pant-blow, blowing during 15-second peaks.

3 pushing contractions—push 10 seconds, three times per contraction.

Kegel Exercises

Continue daily exercises in your routine as before.

Express complementary air when tired.

Push properly when having a bowel movement, releasing muscles in the pelvic floor.

Topics for Discussion and Action

1. Complete the Readiness Test on the following pages. How well did you do? In what areas do you need to improve?

READINESS TEST

After your fifth childbirth class, take this test. It will give you a fair indication of your progress. Have the coach give you as many points per question as he thinks you deserve. Remember, coach, be objective!

Conditioning	POSSIBLE SCORE	YOUR SCORE
1. Have you discussed with your coach your feelings about your pregnancy and labor?	5	_____
2. Have you and your coach role-played different situations that could arise during labor?	5	_____
3. Do you and your coach understand the body mechanics of labor?	8	_____
4. Do you and your coach understand the Lamaze theory?	5	_____
5. Have you called a contraction "pain" at any time during the past week?	5	_____

6. Have you practiced both release and breathing techniques every day during the past week? (Twice-a-day or more, add 5 bonus points.) .... 8 _____
7. Has the coach practiced with you at least once a day? .... 6 _____
8. Do you practice releasing and breathing when you have Braxton-Hicks contractions? .... 5 _____

Breathing

1. Are you able to perform deep chest breathing? .... 5 _____
2. Can you accelerate and decelerate smoothly at all breathing levels? ...... 5 _____
3. Have you hyperventilated (dizziness, tingling limbs, etc.) during a practice session at any time this week? .... 5 _____
4. Can you fast-pant rhythmically for 20 seconds while well released? .... 5 _____
5. Can you pant-blow for 60 seconds while well released? .... 5 _____
6. Have you mastered the steps to pushing? .... 4 _____
   a) Do you tense your face while pushing? .... 8 _____
7. Are you able to correct your breathing according to your coach's commands? . 8 _____

Neuromuscular Release

1. Are you able to contract and release any muscle group covered thus far *immediately* upon command? .... 10 _____
2. Have you and your coach discussed techniques and experimented to find the best way he can help relieve your tension? .... 6 _____
3. Are you aware of unnecessary tension in

your body during the day? Do you
release it? .... 5 _____
4. Can you "release away" discomfort? ... 5 _____

There are 100 points possible, plus an additional 5 bonus points.

YOUR SCORE

Above 85—You are well prepared for a rewarding childbirth experience. Keep up the good work!

Above 75—You are fairly well prepared, but need to work on any weak points.

Above 65—You need work in all areas.

Below 65—You need intensive work in all areas above—beyond the suggested practice session.

If your score was not as high as you had hoped, don't worry. There is still time to raise it with more practice. If you feel it's hopeless, talk to your instructor. She can provide extra help.

CHAPTER 8

And Baby Makes Three

A threefold cord is not quickly broken. (Eccles. 4:12)

THE LANGUAGE OF LOVE

The greatest love in the world is depicted in the Greek word *agape*. It is used to describe the type of love God has for us, His children. The essence of agape love is *giving*—giving with no thought of receiving anything in return.

The love between a husband and wife is often a beautiful example of agape love. But an even more profound demonstration of this is seen in the affection parents have for their children. Nowhere else is loving devotion given so profusely to someone with so little to give in return.

Parents will readily admit how much they love their children. Yet many have a difficult time actually showing this love to them. They need to understand what means "love" to a child. Fortunately, the Lord has given each tiny baby everything he needs to receive and understand messages of love from his parents:

He has skin. Touch him. Caress him. Did you ever feel anything so soft in your whole life? Stroke his cheek, his tiny earlobe, his little bottom. They *invite* touching! *Touch* is the first language infants begin to understand. The sense of touch is better developed at birth than any of the other senses. Through touch he is able to learn of the world around him. He learns about textures, shapes, sounds and smells. He begins to detect your attitudes and moods. He learns that someone "is there."

Many first-time parents are afraid to cuddle and hold their new baby, usually because he seems so frail. But that tiny frame is really quite sturdy, and the baby's smallness is really another indication that he is *meant* to be held—such convenient packaging!

Look at his eyes. They are magnificent—captivating! A baby's eyes are nearly full grown at birth. No one can deny that a major part of a baby's appeal is his large, expressive eyes that seem to reveal his very soul. Eye contact is a very special way to demonstrate love to your baby. Studies are now proving what many mothers thought they knew all along: babies *can* see things at birth, and they are able to focus on things at a very early age. They will even *prefer* to look at another pair of eyes rather than other objects. Babies are designed for lots of eye contact.

He is helpless. What a test of *giving*! He relies on you for everything. He cannot change his diapers. He cannot burp by himself. He cannot roll over. Often he can't even control his head movements. Although he doesn't know much about being grateful to those who wait on him hand and foot, he *must* be getting the idea that he is precious to someone. And indeed he is! Aren't you glad you can *show* him?

YOUR BABY FROM HEAD TO TOE

Many parents are unprepared for the appearance and behavior of their newborn. Problems or questions which may seem elementary to a doctor or experienced parent may be a source of worry to a new mother or father. Below are some things that often concern new parents, descriptions of what is usually normal, and guidelines for small problems.

Arms—Often drawn up against chest, with fists clenched tightly. Hands sometimes seem large. The skin of the hands and wrists is wrinkly and often becomes somewhat dry and flaky during the first week or so. Nails are thin, and soft, yet sharp.

Body—Not at all like a "miniature adult's"! A baby has features all his own—a full, rounded abdomen, narrow hips, short neck. Babies frequently curl up into the "fetal position" they liked best before birth.

Bowel movements—The first stools after birth are thick and tarlike, and are called "meconium." Within a few days these change to softer, yellowish stools. They may be very runny or somewhat pasty in consistency. It is not uncommon to have a bowel movement with every diaper change at first. These become less frequent as the baby's system matures. In the totally breast-fed baby the odor is mild, and eventually he may have much longer periods between movements—as many as seven days. This is still normal.

Breasts—Hormones from the mother's system may cause the breasts of both boys and girls to be slightly swollen at birth. Sometimes a milky substance referred to as "witch's milk" may even be present. These conditions usually last only a few days, and in many babies do not occur at all.

Breathing—Often rather irregular and raspy or rattling. This is due to mucus still present in the mouth or nose. Breathing is shallow—35-50 breaths per minute (almost a slow pant!).

Circumcision—Change his diaper frequently to keep area dry and prevent irritation. If the area is not wrapped with gauze, you may wish to apply petroleum jelly to the site for 24-36 hours to keep it from sticking to the diaper. If he goes more than 3-4 hours without urinating, or if bleeding occurs beyond a slight tinge, you should notify the doctor. Be careful about laying the baby on his stomach or holding him tightly against you during the first couple of days, unless it doesn't seem to bother him.

"Cold" symptoms—Often, in the newborn, sneezing, coughing, and raspy breathing are simply due to mucus in the respiratory tract. And totally breastfed babies rarely catch colds early in life. However, if it does seem to be a "real" cold, you may wish to keep a vaporizer running near the baby. Keep the room at a moderate temperature—neither too hot nor too cold. You may be successful at removing some of the mucus from the baby's nose by using an infant syringe. If he seems to have difficulty breathing while feeding, you might try feeding him in a steam-filled room (the bathroom works best).

Colic—Spasms of abdominal cramps in the young baby, causing severe crying spells. He usually draws his knees up because of the pain, and may also pass gas. The cause of colic is unknown; in the bottle-fed baby it may be due to intolerance of a certain formula. In the breastfed baby it does not occur as frequently, but it may sometimes be traced to an excessive intake of dairy products by the mother. Walking, rocking, or use of a "baby carrier" that holds him close to you may help to quiet him. Also, massaging his tummy, or placing him on his tummy across your knees can help. Placing a warm towel (straight out of the dryer) under him may help him to sleep. Colic usually disappears between six weeks and three months of age.

Coloring—Immediately after birth, the baby may be slightly blue. This usually changes to a ruddy, mottled appearance soon. When he cries hard his color may turn *deep* red. Sometimes, a few days after birth the skin will become somewhat yellowish, indicating that the body is breaking down extra red blood cells acquired at birth. This normal, physiologic jaundice usually subsides on its own in a few days. You should offer liquids frequently (breast milk is fine, if you're nursing). If the condition persists beyond a few days, contact the doctor.

Cradle cap—This is a thick, brownish flaking of the scalp. Wash hair daily and brush it vigorously, or apply baby oil and comb thoroughly with a fine-tooth comb. If the condition does not disappear with one of these methods, ask the doctor to prescribe a special soap for cradle cap.

Crying—This can be very nerve-wracking, but is rather typical behavior for the newborn! It seems to taper off considerably after about six weeks of age. Other pages in this book discuss crying and possible solutions in greater detail.

Diaper rash—This problem is sometimes caused by a food or formula allergy, but in the breastfed infant, it is almost always due to laundering technique. Try changing to a milder soap and rinsing an extra time.

Diarrhea—True diarrhea is frequent, runny, foul-smelling, and often greenish in appearance. The baby should receive frequent fluids to prevent dehydration. Contact your doctor if it persists more than a day. Remember that the stools of the breastfed baby are normally soft and frequent.

Eyes—Almost all babies have blue-gray eyes at birth. The lids may be puffy from the journey of birth. Babies can see, and can often even focus on a bright-colored object or another pair of eyes. You will find him cross-eyed frequently, since he doesn't have much control of them at first.

Face—A baby usually has full and round cheeks, a broad, flat nose, and sometimes hardly any chin or jaw at first. New babies make some of the funniest expressions imaginable!

Genitals—These are often enlarged at birth. In boys the scrotum may appear very large, as will the vulva in girls. Sometimes girls will even have a spot or two of blood from the vagina. All these conditions are due to maternal hormones and will soon normalize.

Hair—A baby's hair is wet and dark-looking at birth. Many babies lose all their original hair and grow more that is totally different in color and texture. Hair is sometimes rubbed off by sleeping on one side of the head all the time. This is not harmful (it will grow back), though it may look a little strange.

Head—The baby's head may be greatly misshapen or elongated at first, due to the pressure of the birth canal. This is called "molding" and the shape usually returns to normal within a few days. There are two "fontanels" or soft spots—one at the top of the head and one at the back. The back one closes within a few months, and the top one closes usually by 18-24 months. Your baby cannot support his head alone until he is about three months old.

Legs—Legs are bowed, often drawn up into the intrauterine position. They are not much longer than the baby's arms at first. The feet are tiny and wrinkled, and may have some flaking of the skin as the hands do. The foot "bones" are mostly just cartilage.

Pulse—The baby's heart beats 90-160 times a minute. When he cries it can speed up to 180-200 times per minute.

Reflexes—Your baby will suck on anything, and gag, cough and sneeze reflexively. He will turn his head toward a touch and "root" for his food source, swallow, startle easily, grasp whenever his palm is touched, and demonstrate a "stepping" reflex.

Size—Most newborns are 18-20 inches long and weigh 6-8 pounds, the average being 7-7½ pounds. Usually a baby will lose a few ounces during the first few days, but regain that weight within two weeks.

Skin—At birth, most babies have on their skin traces of *vernix caseosa*, a creamy, cheeselike substance which "waterproofs" the baby before birth. This can be rubbed into the skin to serve as a natural "coldcream." Fine, downy hair called *lanugo* may also be present on the face, shoulders, arms, but this soon disappears. Many babies have small white bumps across the nose and forehead (called *milia*), but these will also go away with no treatment.

Sleep—Some babies sleep for long stretches without waking; others sleep fitfully, waking frequently. Both patterns are normal, and babies usually settle into more predictable sleep habits by three months or so.

Spitting up—Occurs frequently in the young baby. Can be caused by excessive air swallowed during feeding, by crying hard prior to feeding, or by sucking on an empty bottle. The force of a mother's let-down reflex may also cause the baby to gulp and choke and subsequently swallow air. To minimize the swallowing of air, try to feed the baby when he is still calm, not frantically screaming for a meal. Also, hold him at about a 45-degree angle while he eats and burp him frequently.

Temperature—At birth, normal temperature is about 96 degrees rectally, but when well stabilized it is closer to 99.6. Babies do not perspire at first, but will develop a heat rash instead.

Umbilical cord—The stump will dry up, turn black, and drop off in 7-14 days. Before it falls off, keep navel dry and sponge with alcohol three times daily. If you notice excessive bleeding, redness, or an odor in the area, the doctor should be consulted.

Urination—Urine should be clear or pale yellow. If a baby has at least 6-8 wet diapers a day he is considered normal, but most have many more! If you are concerned about whether or not he is getting enough milk, this "output" is a good measuring stick, provided you are not offering water or supplements.

When to call the doctor: According to Niles Newton, author of *The Family Book of Child Care*, you should contact your doctor if your baby shows any of the following symptoms:

1. A temperature of 101 or more, even with no other symptoms. Suspect fever if your child is flushed or has hot, dry skin. Take temperature with a rectal thermometer lubricated with petroleum jelly.
2. A temperature of 100 or more accompanied by stiff neck or hoarseness.
3. Convulsions, twitching, or general muscle spasms.
4. Any persistent abdominal pain.
5. Extremes of behavior that are not normal for the child: irritability, loss of appetite, listlessness, unconsciousness.

6. Swelling, redness, throbbing pain in any injured part of the body.

The following symptoms may or may not turn into real illness. You should phone the doctor if they are persistent:

1. Irritability and crying.
2. Drowsiness and excessive desire to sleep.
3. Temperature between 100 and 101 without stiffness or hoarseness.
4. Vomiting.
5. Diarrhea.
6. Runny nose.
7. Cough.
8. Sore throat.
9. Frequent sneezing.
10. Real pain anywhere throughout the body.
11. Rash or skin eruption.[1]

WHEN BABY'S CRYING GETS TRYING*

by Niles Newton, Ph.D.

Your baby is crying. He has just been fed and diapered, but still he is fussing. What do you do next to quiet him?

Your baby is asking for something. The key questions are: Is your baby in physical discomfort? Is he missing the constant contact, the rhythmic heartbeat sound, and the physical joggling he got in the womb? Could your baby be bored, wanting a greater variety of sights and sounds?

Physical discomforts—Physical discomforts are often the easiest to remedy. Here are some practical measures:

Some babies fuss while they are having a bowel movement. It sometimes helps to give an infant's feet something firm to push on to help the process. Try holding him up over your shoulder as you walk back and forth, and place your second hand on the sole of his feet so he can push against it.

Sometimes an air bubble in the tummy is uncomfortable and has prevented the baby from eating as much as he would like.

*© 1977 La Leche League, Int'l. Reprinted by permission.

One easy way of bubbling or burping your baby is to lay him across your crossed knees, holding his abdomen with one hand while his head rests against your arm. With the other hand gently rub his back with an upward motion. After this another suck at the breast may be appreciated.

Dirty and wet diapers do not bother many babies unless they have sore bottoms or have been trained by a meticulous mother to expect the constant dry feel. Mild soap and many rinses should be used on home-washed diapers, with enough changing to help forestall diaper rash.

If rash develops, try leaving off the diapers, soakers, and plastic altogether. Free circulation of air helps skin healing, and a baby usually loves it. When he needs to be socially acceptable, wrap a receiving blanket around his bottom but not between his legs.

Other physical discomforts may involve feeling too hot or too cold or wanting more feeding even though some has been obtained. Sometimes you are more hungry than other times, and babies are equally variable.

"Missing the Womb"—Another cause of fussing is what I like to call "missing the womb fuss." Baby finds it comforting to have some of the conditions he experienced for most of his life restored to him, particularly during the first weeks after birth.

Before birth your baby has heard the steady beat, beat, beat of your heart, which may make him appreciative of rhythmic sounds. Lullabies are used the world over, and radio, record players, and cassette tape recorders make it easy to supply sounds.

Your baby has also felt warmth and snugness in the womb, so that wrapping blankets tightly around him, swaddling him, is sometimes comforting. If you are placing him on his side, put a rolled blanket behind his back, since he cannot at first control his own wiggling and flopping and gets upset by his own unrestrained sprawling.

The time-honored tradition of rocking the baby to sleep is very effective. Rocking chairs and rocking baby beds have a long history. The rocking chair has an advantage, since both mother and baby may get soothed at the same time.

Some mothers, especially those who are breastfeeding, go

back to the ways of their great-great-grandmother when faced with a fussy baby at night. Many old medical textbooks emphasize the need for the baby to be comforted by sleeping with his mother.

One way of sleeping with a baby is to have your arm curled around him. Another very comforting way is to place the baby on your chest with his tummy against yours. Pat or rub him gently until he quiets down.

If the bed seems a bit crowded, consider a king-sized bed. Some couples prefer to have a mattress on the floor for mother and baby while they sleep and nurse. When baby goes to sleep, he is left on the mattress and mother goes back to bed with her husband.

When baby is bored—Another form of fussing is the "I want to be up and around" type of cry. Babies do get bored, and since they cannot move themselves to interesting sights and sounds, their only way of helping themselves is to fuss for attention.

Although this kind of fussing can happen at many times of the day, it is most usually in the late afternoon when Mother is busy cooking supper and getting ready for Father's return, and when other children may be demanding extra attention.

One of the best solutions to this is a baby carrier that holds the baby against the mother's chest. The framed kind of carriers used on the back are not as comforting for a new baby, who likes to be held close to his mother's heart, feeling her body very close to his.

Another way of giving variety and stimulation is to take a bath with your baby. It is restful for both of you, and the baby usually loves the skin contact with his mother.

An air bath also sometimes delights a baby. Lying on his back with all his clothes off, he can have the fun of kicking unrestricted. When he tires of this, place him on his tummy so he can lift his head and look around.

Fathers and neighbors and relatives can be a great help to a harried mother by giving her a "half hour break" to regain her energy. While she takes a little rest and freshens up, others can take the baby on a tour of the house, talking to him and letting him see each room.

Taking the baby outdoors to see the bright sky and new objects sometimes works wonders, and if extra soothing is required, a car ride may have remarkable quieting results.

Babies are not as conventional as adults. Sometimes they like to look at the floor instead of being held upright. One of my favorite quieting positions is to place the baby lying face downward on my knees looking at the floor. Gentle rocking can be accomplished by lifting one heel and then the other.

Comforting a fussing baby does take time, because often what baby is demanding is "more of mother." But babies grow up rapidly. Although his demands may seem excessive at first, given a few months more you may be hankering for a tiny one again.

BENEFITS OF BREASTFEEDING

For Mother:
1. Breastfeeding is delightfully convenient: no bottles and nipples, no sterilizing, no formula to mix and warm, no extra consideration for trips or outings.
2. If you breastfeed right after the birth, you are less likely to hemorrhage. Hormones are released during nursing which cause the uterus to remain contracted, thus closing the wound where the placenta was attached.
3. It inhibits ovulation—natural child spacing! Of course, this decreased fertility is only temporary and should not be relied upon solely as a form of contraception.
4. It helps you regain your figure more quickly; your baby will consume hundreds of calories daily.
5. There is some evidence that women who have breastfed have less chance of getting breast cancer.
6. You are not left to do housework while someone else feeds the baby. You get a guilt-free break every time you breastfeed the baby.
7. It's less expensive. There is no getting around the fact that formulas *cost money*! There is also the expense of bottles, nipples, and sterilizers.
8. Breastfed babies are more pleasant to be around. They don't have the strong smell that is often associated with bottle-fed babies.
9. Breastfeeding is an intensely pleasureable, sensual expe-

rience. It makes for an easier transition from childbirth to sex relations; women who nurse are emotionally ready to resume sex much sooner than non-nursing mothers.

10. The knowledge that you are giving your baby something no one else can, creates a tie between you and your child that can become one of your deepest joys. Many women consider the nursing months among the most fulfilling times of their lives.

For Baby:

1. Generally speaking, people who have been breastfed enjoy better health. They have fewer cavities, fewer allergies, and are less prone to become overweight.
2. Breast milk is full of antibodies and immunities that protect the baby from many sicknesses and diseases.
3. Breast milk is easier to digest than formula. Thus, the baby is less likely to be colicky.
4. Fully breastfed babies do not become anemic in the first four to six months. Bottle-fed babies may become anemic, even with iron supplements.
5. There is no time wasted in preparation. When the baby is hungry, the milk is ready. There is no waiting.
6. Breastfeeding enhances cuddling, carressing, and touching in a way that cannot be matched in bottle-feeding (It's too easy to prop a bottle.).

We believe that breastfeeding is the superior way to feed your baby. It creates an environment conducive to good mothering. In itself, however, breastfeeding does not necessarily make one a good mother; nor does bottle-feeding make a woman a bad mother. Our intent is to provide you with the information to make an educated decision. Even if you do not breastfeed, knowing about it may make you a better neighbor or friend to someone who does.

NIPPLE CARE*

DURING PREGNANCY

You may or may not run into any difficulty with your nipples

---

*Adapted from *The Womanly Art of Breastfeeding*, LaLeche League, Int'l. Used by permission.

if you give them no special care during pregnancy. Many women who don't bother with any special preparations beforehand never have any trouble with sore nipples, no matter how long or how strongly their babies nurse. However, some women, especially redheads and others with fair complexions, do have difficulty with tenderness or soreness; and since you can't tell ahead of time, it is wise to follow a few simple preparatory routines.

Your regular bath is all the washing the nipples will require, now or later. Go easy on the soap. Many of us eliminate soap entirely for a while in bathing the nipple area. If you must use it, do so sparingly and rinse well, because soap is drying to the skin and dryness encourages cracked nipples.

A daily routine. It's well to devote some time to conditioning the nipples during the last several weeks of pregnancy. When you are dressing and undressing are good times to remember to do a couple of simple exercises. For instance, you might rub your nipples gently with a turkish towel. You could also pull them out with your fingers several times, quite firmly. (Some mothers use a lubricant, such as cold cream or baby oil.) Do any such rubbing or pulling only until it is slightly uncomfortable, never to the point of pain. Such exercises take only a few minutes. The important thing is to be regular about doing them.

It is also helpful to go without a bra part of each day (or, if that is uncomfortable for you, you could wear a nursing bra and drop the trap door), in order to expose the nipples to the air and the gentle friction of your outer clothing.

Hand-expression. It is sometimes suggested that you hand-express a few drops of colostrum from each breast every day during the last six weeks of pregnancy, and you may want to do this, with your doctor's approval. Colostrum is the fluid secreted before the milk comes in, which doctors say is so important for the newborn baby and one good reason (there are others) why you should nurse your baby as soon after delivery as possible. The reason for expressing the colostrum daily for a few weeks before the baby is born is that some think it tends to open the milk ducts, thereby reducing the engorgement which sometimes occurs when the milk first comes in and which some mothers find quite uncomfortable.

If you do decide to try hand-expressing colostrum, you can add it to your regular nipple-conditioning routine.

Hand-expression is quite simple. It is the same whether you are expressing a few drops of colostrum during the last weeks of pregnancy or milk later on. Cup the breast in your hand, placing your thumb above and forefinger below the nipple on the edge of the dark area (areola). Press inward toward the chest wall, squeeze thumb and finger together gently, release and repeat. Don't slide the thumb and finger out toward the nipple. Rotate your hand to reach all the milk ducts, which radiate out from the nipple at all points of the clock. Alternate sides every few minutes. Be sure to do it *very gently*, and only once or twice a day. It may take quite a while to get any colostrum at all; some mothers never do. But don't worry—it'll be there when your baby nurses.

Inverted nipples. If you have flat or inverted nipples, you may not be able to carry out the recommended nipple care as easily as the mother with protruding nipples; but work at it and eventually you will find you can manage. A little practice now will save a lot of time and maybe some mental anguish after the baby is born. One mother who has this kind of nipple has called it "the folding model of the nipple world"; there is a real full-sized nipple there, ready and able to do the job for which it was intended, but it folds back into the breast when not in use. Completely inverted nipples are quite rare, and they can be a nuisance. On the other hand, rather flat, even depressed nipples, which are quite common, respond to the kind of treatment suggested above. You may not be able to decide which kind you have. If you suspect that you may have an inverted nipple, pinch the areola between the forefinger and thumb just behind the base of the nipple (as in hand-expression) and see what happens. If it reacts by coming out, even a little, this is not a true inverted nipple. Even though you may not be able to get it out very far now, the baby will later on.

If the nipples react to this pressure by retreating (exceptional, but it sometimes happens), then you do have inverted nipples, and you will have to work a little harder to get them in condition for nursing, because you won't be able to grasp them. The thing is, you have to get them out some for the baby to be able to latch on. Once he can take hold, he will carry on from there.

The best treatment for bringing out truly inverted nipples is the use of breast shields* designed for this purpose, worn during pregnancy before the baby is born.

AFTER BABY COMES

If nipples are hard to grasp. Sometimes a mother may discover after the baby is born that she has an inverted nipple she didn't suspect, or, more often, her nipples may be temporarily retracted because of engorgement. When it is engorgement that is causing the difficulty, usually hand-expressing a little milk (see page 113) will bring the nipple out.

The special breast shields* may be useful at this time, too, worn between feedings. If it's simply engorgement, just the times between two feedings may do the trick. In more severe cases it may be necessary to wear them for a day or two or even for two or three weeks. *The mother should not save the milk that leaks into the shields to feed the baby*, and she is advised to wash the shields frequently with hot soapy water, rinse thoroughly, and dry carefully. She should try to leave the nipples exposed to the air for fifteen to thirty minutes several times each day.

Sometimes, even though there is no problem of inverted nipples or engorgement, a mother may have quite soft, small nipples, and the young baby may open his mouth and shake his head back and forth at the breast trying to locate the nipple. Placing a cold, wet cloth on the nipple for a few seconds, causing the areola to shrivel and the nipple to protrude and become firm, is usually all that is needed.

If your nipples get sore. Sore nipples aren't an illness, but they *can* be very uncomfortable. They may become tender, and

---

*These *breast shields* should not be confused with *nipple shields*, which have rubber nipples that go over the real nipples and are sometimes used for a different purpose, while the baby is nursing. The *breast shields* are in two sections; the bottom part fits over the breast, with a hole for the nipple, and the top part does not touch the nipple but holds the bra away from it and catches any leakage. They are used before the baby is born, or between feedings afterward, never while the baby is nursing.

in some few cases even cracked or bleeding, in spite of prenatal care. If they do, exposing them to the air is a very effective way to help to heal them. If you can do so in comfort, eliminate wearing your bra as much as possible and wear a soft, loose blouse. Otherwise, make sure the bra is not tight; you might also drop the trap door in the bra and leave it open as much as you can. Another suggestion which has worked well for some mothers is to remove the handles from tea strainers and insert the strainers inside your bra cups to keep the clothing from irritating the nipples and permit circulation of air around them.

Any mild ointment prescribed for you may help. While most do not contain ingredients which could be harmful to the baby, be sure to read the label for instructions about removing before putting baby to the breast. Vaseline, pure lanolin, or A & D Ointment are among those which are usually safe, but lanolin could cause problems if mother or baby are sensitive to wool. Any ointment that is used should be applied *sparingly*, as it tends to keep out the air and sunlight so important to healing.

Another simple measure that has been suggested is the application of ice or ice water. Those who have tried it say that it eases pain immediately and has the added advantage of helping bring out soft, small nipples or nipples of engorged breasts, as mentioned above. The method is simply to crush ice, wrap it in a washcloth, and apply to the nipple area. The more severe the irritation, the longer the application. It can be used all day if necessary, or during the night, with a towel or waterproof cover below to catch the drip.

It has been our experience that alcohol, tincture of benzoin, and similar drying agents and soap tend to be irritating, so avoid using any of these things. Some mothers have had allergic reactions to detergent residues in their laundered bras, and have had good results from using disposable nursing pads, or more economically, disposable diapers cut into nine sections, with the plastic backing removed. Avoid plastic-coated pads in your bras; they can cause trouble especially in hot weather, by holding in moisture and keeping out air; occasionally mothers have developed a rash from contact of the plastic with the skin.

If soreness persists even after the above suggestions have been tried, a sunlamp may be used. Mothers in tropical climates, whose breasts are customarily exposed to sun and air, don't seem to have sore nipples. Some doctors try to duplicate this by ultraviolet ray sunlamp on the breasts. An expensive lamp is not necessary; you can buy an ultraviolet bulb and put it in any lamp stand or socket. Sitting three feet from the lamp, expose yourself no more than one-half minute the first day, one minute the second and third days, two minutes the fourth and fifth days. If there is no indication of skin reddening by this time, you may increase to three minutes on the sixth day and maintain that level once a day until the soreness is gone. If you do notice a redness at two minutes, cut down to one minute and continue at that level for several days. Then try gradually increasing, one-half minute at a time, to see if you can tolerate a longer period. If not, keep it at the level that is best for you.

Be extremely careful always to protect your eyes with a towel or other cover while you are using the lamp; be careful about handling the bulb after use—it gets very hot; be careful not to get a sunburn from the lamp. It is imperative that you time yourself with a clock or watch.

Some mothers think that nursing less often—say every four hours instead of two or three—will help sore nipples. The opposite is more often true. Easy-going, leisurely nursing every two or three hours is actually easier on nipples that are tender, because then the breasts don't become overfull, and the baby doesn't get so ravenously hungry that he nurses over-vigorously.

There is possibly a relation between apprehension on the part of the mother and sore nipples. Slightly tender nipples may cause enough tension to hold back the let-down reflex. The delay in the milk may make the baby angry so that he pulls and tugs on the nipple, making it even sorer—and creating greater concern on your part. What can you do about this? You can hand-express a little milk to start the flow; and you can make a deliberate effort to relax before nursing. Try a warm tub or shower, or quicker and sometimes even more effective, lean over a washbowl with breasts immersed in comfortably hot water.

Some doctors prescribe a pain relieving medication during the time your nipples may be painfully tender. *Consult your doctor in this matter.* It also helps to change your position at each feeding, to put the greatest pressure in different places. Sit up for one feeding, lie down for the next.

Sore nipples are sometimes caused by a fungus infection, perhaps in connection with thrush in the baby. You suspect thrush (a fairly common condition, bothersome but not serious) if soreness persists, especially if there are white spots inside the baby's mouth, or if he has persistent diaper rash, or you develop vaginitis. Another situation in which you suspect fungus infection is if you suddenly develop sore nipples after several weeks or months of clear sailing. Call your doctor's attention to any of these symptoms. Treatment is simple, and there's no need to stop nursing.

During the time the nipples are quite sore, it may be necessary to limit the nursing time to ten minutes on each side. This will provide the baby with all the nourishment he needs. Studies have shown he'll get nearly 90 percent of the milk in the first seven minutes. However, this may not satisfy all his *sucking* needs, especially if he has been nursing for longer periods. A pacifier may be helpful here, but don't try to substitute the pacifier for Mother. Continue to hold him at least as long as you would if he were nursing for the usual time so as to satisfy both his sucking need and his need of you. The one-piece rubber pacifier with a wide flange is safest. As soon as the nipples heal, go back to the full nursing period and discontinue the use of the pacifier. Limited use at this early age will not establish a habit or interfere with the baby's oral development, but it may be difficult to establish a good nursing pattern if he relies on the pacifier for a considerable amount of sucking satisfaction.

Some mothers have given up nursing because of sore nipples. This is unfortunate because it isn't necessary. The nipples can be treated in the way we have described while you continue nursing, and the soreness will usually persist only for a few days. In the few very rare cases of extremely sore nipples, which might occur if there has been no preparation before the baby is born and no treatment of beginning tenderness, it may be necessary to discontinue breastfeeding temporarily. During this time the mother may have to hand-express her milk and give it to the baby from a dropper or a spoon. As soon as the nipples respond to treatment, the baby can be put back on the breast.

WHAT TO EAT WHILE BREASTFEEDING

The nursing mother needs a superior diet to meet the baby's

nutritional needs, as well as her own. Many postpartum problems can be reduced or eliminated through proper nutrition. A mother should never "diet" during lactation.

The following is a food guide for breastfeeding mothers. Using it will insure intake of essential nutrients to meet their metabolic needs:

Daily Food Guide[2]

Food Group	Number of Servings
Protein foods	4
Milk and milk products	5
Whole grain products	3
Vitamin C-rich fruits and vegetables	1
Leafy green vegetables	2
Other fruits and vegetables	1

In addition, daily supplements of folacin (400-800 I.U.) and iron (30-60 mg.) are recommended.

The above guide may not meet the caloric needs of the lactating woman. For that reason, additional foods should be included in her diet to raise the caloric count *1500 calories* above her pre-pregnancy diet.

Eat heartily but healthfully. Avoid rich, calorie-laden desserts and heavy pastas. This allows weight reduction without energy reduction, and will not affect the baby's nutrition.

Spicy foods or "gassy" foods (such as cabbage and beans) may upset your baby's stomach. They need not be ruled out of your diet completely, but use them with caution. Also there is growing evidence that excessive intake of milk and dairy products by a nursing mother may cause "colic" in her baby. If you notice a reaction in your baby after you have eaten such a food, eliminate that particular item from your diet. Coffee and tea may also make a baby wakeful or irritable.

Be sure to drink lots of fluids. It is not necessary to drink excessively large amounts, but do make sure that you never feel "thirsty." Many women feel an intense thirst at nursing time,

COMMON BREASTFEEDING PROBLEMS AND WHAT TO DO

The chart below is in no way a substitute for the personal experience and friendly advice to be offered by your childbirth instructor or a La Leche League leader. Either will be happy to help you at any hour of the day or night. However, should you be unable to find help, these pages contain some of the most common problems mothers experience, and some possible solutions. Sometimes just knowing that a problem is "normal" makes it seem smaller and easier to deal with.

PROBLEM	POSSIBLE CAUSES	THINGS TO REMEMBER	WHAT TO DO	ADDITIONAL INFORMATION
Engorgement—full, uncomfortable breasts.	On 3rd-5th day postpartum, caused by breasts getting ready to *work*.	You won't always be this big—it goes away soon. Baby may have a hard time grasping nipple; squeeze it between two fingers.	Nurse *frequently* to prevent or reduce. Apply heat or cold if desired.	*Eiger & Olds, p. 151 *WABF, pp. 28, 55 100, 103
Sore or cracked nipples.	Nipples unprepared for baby's strong suction. Sometimes due to baby being nursed infrequently in hospital.	They need *air* to heal. Nurse baby frequently to prevent him from becoming ravenously hungry and sucking so hard.	Avoid creams and lubricants that will block exposure to air. Keep them dry. Expose to air as much as possible (fold down flaps of bra). Expose to sunlight or sunlamp (30 sec. only).	Eiger & Olds, pp. 148-50 *Pryor, pp. 179-81 WABF, pp. 98-101 *LLLI Reprint #12
Leaking.	Breasts still "learning" how to function, often overproduce at first. Thoughts of baby can trigger let-down reflex.	This will diminish greatly after first six weeks or so. It is a temporary condition.	Make your own washable nursing pads out of flannel, handkerchiefs, old T-shirts, etc.—saves money! Applying pressure directly to nipple will stop let-down reflex.	Eiger & Olds, pp. 71, 116 Pryor, pp. 176-77 WABF, pp. 78-79

*References are to the following books: Eiger & Olds, *The Complete Book of Breastfeeding*, Bantam Books; Pryor, *Nursing Your Baby*, Pocket Books, *The Womanly Art of Breastfeeding* (WABF), La Leche League International. La Leche League reprints are available from the national headquarters (see resource list) or from your local La Leche League leader.

Milk supply decreasing.	*Maybe it isn't*—after engorgement goes away your breasts feel smaller and less full and hard. *Maybe it is*—are you offering water or formula? Are you feeding solids? These things will decrease production.	Increased nursing will build up supply; offering *any* substitutes will decrease it. A hungry baby tells breasts to produce more; satisfying the baby with supplements will make them "think" they're producing enough.	Feed baby on demand. Offer both breasts each time. To build up supply, offer every 1-2 hours for a couple of days. Get lots of rest. Give *nothing* but breast. Eat and drink as much as possible.	Eiger & Olds, pp. 105-107, 154 Pryor, pp. 29-34 WABF, pp. 64-66, 68, 95-97 LLLI Reprint #83
Baby hungry all the time.	He may be having a "growth spurt," and needs to nurse more often to increase your production. These occur most commonly at 4 days, 2 wks., 6 wks., 3 mos., and 6 mos., with many variations, of course.	If you don't supplement at this time, your supply will increase sufficiently in a day or two. Remember also, breast milk digests so rapidly that the baby may need to eat every hour-or-two some days.	Let him nurse, even if it seems constant and you feel totally "empty." There's always more being produced. In a couple of days your supply will even up with his increased demand.	Eiger & Olds, pp. 103-105 Pryor, pp. 184-85, 224 WABF, pp. 73-74 LLLI Reprints #16, 83
Normally hungry baby refuses to nurse, cries frequently.	Breast too full, nipple hard to grasp. Mother tense, not rested, causing poor let-down. Is his nose stopped up so he can't breathe while nursing? Older baby: possibly teething.	If mother can *relax,* this will help baby to calm down. Even if you can't discover the cause of crying, let your baby know you love him and care. Try not to be impatient!	Hand-express a little to reduce breast size. Squeeze nipple between two fingers to help him grasp. Try nose drops if congestion seems to be the problem. If you can get the baby to *almost* fall asleep, he may take the breast subconsciously.	Eiger & Olds, pp. 155-157, 107-108 Pryor, p. 176 WABF, pp. 62, 104 LLLI Reprint #57

Fussy baby.	Difference in babies' temperaments. May have extra sensitivity to all stimuli. May need extra sucking.	This will smooth out between 6 wks. and 3 mos. If you can remain as calm as possible and keep his environment as free from busy-ness as possible, he will fare better!	Allow baby to nurse freely. If milk supply is sufficient, you may wish to offer a pacifier. Be patient and calm in handling—this too will pass!	Eiger & Olds, pp. 100-103 Pryor, pp. 203, 211, 239 WABF, pp. 71-76 LLLI Reprint #141
Sleepy, disinterested baby.	Difference in babies' temperaments. May be due to medication in labor and birth.	Babies grow at different rates. If he has 6-8 wet diapers a day and is receiving no water, he is eating enough.	Encourage nursing by stroking baby's cheek. Stimulate sucking by touching roof of baby's mouth with fingertip. Offer breast frequently.	Eiger & Olds, pp. 119, 154-155 Pryor, p. 174 WABF, p. 57, 69 LLLI Reprint #104
Breast infection (Mastitis).	Failure of let-down reflex to keep milk flowing smoothly.	It is better to nurse through a breast infection than to quit. Healing will be quicker and long-lasting.	Rest in bed constantly. Apply heat to breast. Nurse frequently (every hour or so).	Eiger & Olds, pp. 152-153 Pryor, pp. 204-206 WABF, pp. 97-98, 101-104 LLLI Reprint #12

just as the milk lets down. This built-in reaction should serve as a reminder to drink a glass of water, juice, or milk for every feeding that your baby has. Then you can be assured of your own needs being met, as well as having plenty of milk for the baby.

WHEN SHOULD YOUR BABY BEGIN SOLID FOODS?

The introduction of solid foods seems to be a milestone in the lives of most babies (and their mothers!). For some reason we have allowed ourselves to be convinced that the earlier a baby begins eating a variety of foods other than breast milk or formula, the more "advanced" he is. The truth is, however, that your baby stands a better chance of a healthy, normal life *without* solids for the first few months.

Breast milk is the perfect food for infants during their first four to six months after birth. By perfect, we mean that it supplies *everything* the baby needs in the proportions he needs: vitamins, minerals, protein, fats, carbohydrates, and calories. When we make additions to his diet, we alter the natural balance of his diet and substitute inferior food for the superior one. If a baby begins to fill up on other foods at an early age, several things will happen: (1) His intake of breast milk or formula will be cut down. (2) The groundwork will be laid for obesity later on in life. (3) He will become more susceptible to allergies because his system is not ready to handle solid foods. All of these things represent health hazards which most of us would rather avoid. It only makes sense to do what we can to see that our children enjoy a happy, healthy childhood.

Even formula-fed babies do not usually *need* solids until three or four months of age. When they are introduced to solids, it should be with great care.

If either parent has any type of allergy history, whether it be food, drug, or pollen, you should especially consider waiting until six months or so to begin with other foods, as your baby is probably more vulnerable to allergies than many. Babies who are *totally* breastfed for the first six months rarely develop allergies of any sort, but even if they do, they have much milder reactions.

How will you know when your baby's need for additional food

begins? He will make it clear to you. If he is past four or five months of age and has an "eating spurt" (he wants to nurse all the time and doesn't seem to be satisfied with what he's getting) and if this doesn't go away within a couple of days, it could be a sign. Be certain, however, that you don't mistake teething or illness for this signal. If it is really solid food he wants, he will be content after eating it. If your baby, at four to six months, begins reaching for and grabbing food off plates at the table, he is probably ready for solids. Once again, make sure it is the food he wants, and not just the thrill of capturing things with his hands!

If you determine that your baby *is* ready for other foods, it is important that you be as cautious about what you feed him as you were about waiting in the first place. You don't have to feed him the item he reached for at the table—he'll be happy with anything, so make sure it is something nutritious that is not combined with any other food (as this might interfere with your ability to decide which food causes an allergic reaction). Some people begin with something rich in iron, like liver, sauteed in a little bit of oil, and cut into finger-size strips. Your baby will get a great thrill out of gnawing it till it's ragged, since he probably is teething at this age too! And in spite of his parents' personal feelings about the taste of liver, if it's presented to him with a smile, he'll eat it with great enjoyment—he's never had any other foods to which he can compare it! If you absolutely cannot fathom giving your baby liver as his first "real food," try some other chewy type of meat, or a whole-grain cereal if you prefer. It is important to make sure your baby has nursed first, however, so that he is still getting his main nourishment from the milk that is so vital in his first year of growth. The purpose of gradual introduction is not to actually *feed* the baby at first, but to get him used to new tastes and textures and to make sure no allergic reactions are occurring.

Once you have introduced a new food, you may repeat it as desired, but you should not try him on another one for at least four to seven days. In this way you can make sure that each food agrees with him. If you notice *any* physical changes, such as a rash, eczema, digestive disturbance, diaper irritation, etc., discontinue the use of that food and see if the problem clears up. If you had coated that previously mentioned piece of liver with wheat flour, then sauteed it in butter, and your baby reacted allergically to it, you would not know the exact cause—it could be the meat (beef), the flour (wheat), or the butter (milk product).

Many pediatricians feel that it is not a good idea to offer wheat, eggs, citrus products, tomatoes, chocolate, or cows' milk before the child's first birthday. These foods seem to be prime suspects in causing early health problems.

Aside from the problem of potential allergies, which is a real enough problem in itself (after all, how many people do you know that aren't allergic to *anything*?), one ought to use common sense in helping a child discover new tastes. If you first feed him a variety of fruits, such as applesauce, pears, peaches and bananas, he will not be too impressed when you begin offering carrots, green beans, and liver. He will be convinced by that time that food has to be sweet to be edible—and the groundwork is thus laid for a sweet tooth and many dental bills in the years to come. Start with iron-rich foods, such as meats, whole grain breads and cereals—*do not* add sugar, jam, or honey to anything! If your child is ready for these foods, he will take them as they are, and will not need "coaxing." Later you can add a variety of brightly colored vegetables, and last of all, fruits.

Does it sound like a lot of work? It does take extra effort to provide your child with high-quality, health-building foods; but the rewards of having a happy, healthy child who loves to eat things that are good for him, plus the bonus of fewer doctor and dental bills, makes the time spent one of your soundest investments.

WORKING TOGETHER

Kegel Step V. As you count to 10, contract the pelvic floor slowly. Hold it tightly for a few seconds. Then slowly release it, counting to 10 again. Repeat several times.

Daily Practice Sessions
Practice twice a day, once with coach, 15 minutes neuromuscular release, interspersed with breathing. Use different positions.

2 60-second contractions—accelerate from slow deep chest to fast deep chest, 15-second peak, decelerate.

2 60-second contractions—accelerate from fast deep chest to medium pant, 20-second peak, decelerate.

2 90-second contractions—accelerate from slow pant to fast pant, 30-second peak, decelerate.

2 60-second contractions—pant-blow.

2 90-second contractions—pant-blow to blow, three 15-second peaks.

3 pushing contractions—push 10 seconds, three times per contraction.

Continue exercises as a part of your daily routine.

Express complementary air.

Don't forget nipple preparation!

Topics for Discussion and Action
1. What do you imagine life with your new baby will be like?
2. How would you react if life turned out to be a lot different from the way you imagined it would be?
3. Discuss your plans for household help and care of the mother after the birth (what type of care will she need and want, and who will provide it?).
4. Once this week, sit down as a couple and plan the baby's homecoming. Discuss your expectations and desires. Determine the best way to achieve your joint expectations.

CHAPTER 9

Getting Back To "Normal"

Put on love, which binds everything together in perfect harmony. (Col. 3:14, RSV)

POSTPARTUM

Your first six weeks after delivery will be a time of learning and a time of recuperation. Life will never be the same again. Once there were two of you, now there are three. You must consider the baby in everything you do. At times the responsibility can be overwhelming. No one ever said that parenting is easy—but the rewards are great. You may be surprised to discover that you aren't overcome with instinctive "mother-love" for your baby. It takes time to learn a new role and time to learn your baby's needs. Don't worry! By the third week you'll know what your baby needs by the difference in his cries. By the sixth week you'll truly feel like a mother, with all the skills and love that are needed.

For 50% of all new mothers, postpartum is laced with periods of depression ("postpartum blues"). If you are depressed on the third day, it is probably due to hormone changes in your body. Many women, especially first-timers, get depressed from a conflict of emotions—they love their babies, but they resent the constant demand and drain such a responsibility entails; resultantly they are filled with guilt and depression. Depression can be minimized by getting lots of rest (fatigue triggers depression), talking everything out with your husband, and getting out of the house (going to the park, going out to eat, etc.).

Physically speaking, you may feel great. Don't let that deceive you, though. You need to take it easy for a while. Cut all housework down to a minimum and spend time on yourself and your baby. Try to rest whenever the baby does. Do exercises and take time for your appearance—nothing will do more for your morale, or your husband's!

> Oh, cleaning and scrubbing can wait till tomorrow,
> But children grow up, I've learned to my sorrow.
> So quiet down, cobwebs; dust, go to sleep;
> I'm rocking my baby and BABIES DON'T KEEP!
>
> © Ruth Hulburt Hamilton
> (Used by permission)[1]

Usually after the first week any discomfort from stitches is over. A hot tub and Sitz baths can help the episiotomy. Remember to continue Kegel exercises. Some couples resume sexual activity by the third or fourth week, but you should check with your doctor concerning this. There may be some pain if the episiotomy is not completely healed. If pain persists, contact your doctor.

Resuming sexual intercourse takes much patience and understanding. During the first two months it may take the new mother much longer to respond to stimulation. Changes in hormones during nursing may also create a need for a lubricant.

Your breasts may leak for a while after the birth. As your breasts become more accustomed to the baby's demands, the leakage should be reduced measurably. Use disposable breast pads or homemade pads (men's handkerchiefs are great) until the leakage is under control. Your nipples may be sore for a while until they toughen up from the baby's sucking. Nurse often. Expose your nipples to the air and sun. Use hydrous lanolin or A & D Ointment until soreness disappears. Be sure to wipe off excess ointment before nursing.

An understanding husband can do much to enhance the postpartum experience. Most of all, his wife needs practical support, encouragement, and approval from a loving husband to turn this experience into a blessed beginning.

For Women Only: COACHES NEED LOVE TOO!

The addition of a new baby to a family brings unbelievable changes. All of us are aware that our priorities in life change occasionally (and usually temporarily) according to the urgent demands of the day. When a family member is sick or incapacitated, for example, there is a greater amount of "giving" on the parts of other family members in order to make the necessary adjustments.

By the same token, when children are small, they require much greater amounts of parents' time and attention than they do as they grow older. A common mistake parents make is allowing the children to become the focal point of their lives, so that the parents begin to lose sight of one another and each other's needs.

A new baby rightfully becomes the center of his parents' attention. He has urgent needs that often only his mother can meet. Everyone is concerned about his welfare and happiness, and this is as it should be. As time goes on, however, the child becomes less dependent and parents should take advantage of this opportunity to renew their marital relationship.

What can be done in the interim? For the first year or so, how can you let your husband know that he is still "Number One," even though much of your time is dominated by the baby? Here are a few suggestions offered by Helen Andelin in *Fascinating Womanhood*:[2]

1. *Listen to him!* Make an effort to spend at least 10-15 minutes a day, just listening. (This may seem like a small time slot, but babies can take up *lots* of your time!) Look at the man behind the words and try to understand his viewpoint.

2. *Accept him.* Before you were married, you wouldn't have thought of changing anything about him. Don't try now. Don't tell him how to be a better father and don't offer him advice on how to improve his life.

3. *Show gratitude* for the happiness he has brought into your life. Greet him with a smile instead of a sigh, and even if you've been busy with the baby all day, try to comb your hair and put on something attractive before he comes home from work.

4. *Put yourself in his shoes!* He has also gained extra responsibility because of the new addition to the family. If he seems edgy or depressed, consider the load that rests on his shoulders and be understanding—he cares about you!

5. *Admire him.* Sure, he knows what you think of him, but there's no harm in telling him over and over how great you think

he is. Be sincere, and be specific—it will mean a lot more.

The key to keeping marriage fresh and alive is *interest.* Be interest*ing* and interest*ed* (in him) and your marriage will flourish.

POSTPARTUM EXERCISES[3]

First Day
1. *Relaxation techniques*
   a. *Prone resting position.* Lie face-down on a firm surface or mattress, with a pillow placed crosswise under your stomach. The pillow should decrease the curve in the low back area, so do not extend it under the hips and thighs. Lie this way as often as possible each day, *to help uterus regain normal position and for relief of low back fatigue.*
   b. *Supine resting position.* Lie on a firm surface on your back, with lower legs resting on a raised, padded surface such as a footstool or several firm pillows. Hips and knees should each be bent at 90-degree angles. If lower back is arched, legs are not elevated high enough. An extra pillow may be placed under the shoulders and head. The purpose of this exercise is *for relaxation and relief of low back and leg fatigue.*
   c. *Twenty second tone-up.* Stand up with shoes off; reach up toward the ceiling. Tighten buttocks and abdominal muscles. Stretch up with one hand and straighten the opposite leg until almost standing on one foot. Then stretch the opposite side. Relax. Repeat frequently throughout the day. *Helps redevelop muscle tone.*
2. *Diaphragmatic breathing.* Begin by lying on your back, knees bent, feet flat on bed or floor. Have two pillows under the shoulders and head. Let one hand rest on the chest and the other on the abdomen, just above waist level.

   Relax, keep mouth closed, and breathe in through nose, swelling the abdomen. Chest should move very little. Now put your teeth together and breathe out slowly making an s-s-s sound. Press inward and upward on the abdomen and contract the abdominal muscles to assist in exhalation. Relax, then repeat. Note that the emphasis is on slow controlled *exhalation*, not inhalation.

When you have mastered this technique while lying down, practice the exercise while sitting, then standing, and finally walking, until it becomes easy and automatic. Begin practicing for 5 minutes at a time. This will help you *regain proper breathing pattern, assist in relaxation, decrease general fatigue, improve abdominal muscle tone.*

3. *Buttock squeeze.* Begin by lying flat on your back. Pinch your buttocks together tightly. Hold for 5 seconds. Relax. Repeat 5 times. This exercise *will help increase muscle tone of buttocks.*

4. *Kegel exercises.* Contract pelvic floor (urethra, vagina, and anus) muscles. Hold 3-5 seconds, then relax. Repeat 10 times. This should be done immediately after the birth and every hour thereafter. Don't be discouraged if at first it seems as if nothing is happening! Your muscles will resume their previous tone if you keep it up. This exercise is important *for aiding the healing of an episiotomy, improving the tone of pelvic floor muscles, controlling bowel and bladder, and helping birth canal regain its original size and elasticity.*

5. *Pelvic realignment*
   a. Lie on back, knees bent, feet flat on floor. Tighten muscles of the lower abdomen and the buttocks so the front of the pelvis tilts upward toward the ribs and your buttocks are raised off the floor slightly. Hold 5 seconds, then relax. Begin with 5 times daily, slowly increasing to 10 times daily.
   b. Standing, tighten buttocks and abdominal muscles to decrease low back curvature. This will aid proper posture and should be practiced frequently throughout the day.
   These exercises will help to *strengthen abdominal muscles and buttocks, improve posture, decrease and prevent low back pain, and provide a basis for proper body mechanics.*

6. *Leg slide exercise.* Start with both knees bent, feet flat on floor. Do exercise 5-a, flattening back against the floor. Hold this position while straightening one leg, sliding heel slowly along floor. Maintain flattened back while bending knee back up (see below). Repeat with other leg. This exercise will *increase abdominal strength for prevention of back fatigue and for proper posture.*

Second and Third Day
Continue exercises 1-6, progressively increasing repetitions.
  7. *Knees-to-chest exercise*
     a. Start by lying on back with knees bent and feet resting on floor. Grasp both hands around right knee and bring slowly to chest. Hold 3 seconds. Return to starting position and repeat with opposite leg.
     b. Assume same starting position as above. Grasp one hand around each knee; bring one knee toward chest and then bring other knee up also. Move knees slightly apart and toward shoulders. Hold 3 seconds. Return to starting position and relax. Repeat several times.

     These exercises will *decrease tightness of lower back and promote good posture.*
  8. *Trunk flexion curl-ups*
     a. Start in same position as above. Let arms rest at your sides. Flatten back against floor. Hold this position and attempt to raise head, shoulders, and upper back slightly off floor. *Do not* sit up completely. Hold 3 seconds while breathing out slowly. Relax. Repeat 5 times.
     b. When "a" is accomplished easily, progress as follows:
        1) arms folded across chest
        2) hands behind neck, elbows pointed forward
        3) hands behind neck, elbows straight out

     These exercises *will strengthen your abdominal muscles.*
  9. *Hip lifts.* Start in same position as above, arms at sides. Tilt pelvis as in 5-a. Raise buttocks, then lower back, then middle back, then upper back until your body is in a straight line from shoulder to knees. Slowly lower the body in reverse sequence. Relax. Repeat 3 times *to strengthen abdomen and promote good posture.*

Fourth and Fifth Day
Continue exercises and activities 1, 2, 4, 7, 8 and 9 with increased repetitions. Discontinue 3, 5, and 6.
10. *Individual leg lifts.* Begin by lying on back, one knee bent, foot on floor and other leg extended straight on floor. Flatten back against floor, keeping knee straight. Raise leg halfway up, then lower it slowly, keeping back flat on floor. Repeat with other leg. *For strengthening abdominal muscles.*

Repeat with other leg. *For strengthening abdominal muscles.*

Sixth Day (15 minutes, once daily). Continue until *at least* six weeks postpartum.

Discontinue exercise 7. Continue other exercises.

11. *Long sitting trunk flexion.* Begin by sitting on floor with legs straight ahead. Put one hand on top of each knee; push knee down and lean chest toward knees, keeping *back straight* and *shoulders back.* Hold 3 seconds. Relax. Repeat. This *will stretch hamstring muscles on back of thighs.*

12. *Chest muscle tone-up*
    a. Lie down on back with knees bent and feet on bed. Extend both arms straight to the side from the shoulders. Keep elbows straight and lift both arms up, touching hands together overhead. Relax and return to starting position. Repeat 15 times.
    b. Hold a one-pound weight in each hand and perform the above exercises, repeating 5-10 times.

    These exercises *will tone the muscles underlying the breasts.*

13. *Upper back extension exercises.* Stand with your back against a wall, knees bent slightly, feet straight ahead, and heels about 6" from the wall. Flatten lower back and neck against wall. Put arms against wall, elbows bent and back of hands touching wall. Start sliding your arms up the wall. Be sure to keep your elbows and backs of hands touching. Slide up as far as you can reach. Hold 3 seconds. Relax and repeat 10 times. This *will strengthen back muscles and muscles between shoulder blades.*

NATURAL FAMILY PLANNING

With so many methods of birth control available today, it seems surprising that any couple should have difficulty finding the one most appropriate for them. And yet many do. The problem seems to lie in the fact that every method has its own drawbacks and most are rather inconvenient. The most "convenient" of all forms seems to be the "pill," yet it is of questionable safety, often has unwelcome side effects, and perhaps most important to new parents, it cannot be taken by nursing mothers.

In recent years new methods have been devised to help women understand their fertility cycles. With this understanding, any couple can detect signs of fertility in the woman and use this knowledge to either achieve a desired pregnancy, or to avoid one by abstaining from intercourse for a short time each month. It is unfortunate that all methods of natural family planning are confused with the "rhythm" method, which is reliable only with about 50% of the female population. In reality, the other methods are highly scientific and accurate, and when used correctly, are equal to, or more effective than, the "pill."

Natural family planning can be achieved by several methods:

1. *Strict temperature method.* This method depends upon abstinence in every cycle until the woman's temperature (taken each day) indicates that the ovulation process is complete and she has entered an infertile period. Requires longer periods of abstinence than some methods.

2. *Combined calendar and temperature method.* Attempts to eliminate some of the abstinence of the early part of the cycle, to allow more "safe" days.

3. *Ovulation (Billings) method.* Based exclusively on the ability of a woman to pinpoint ovulation through changes in the cervical mucus that is present throughout the cycle. Highly effective, and provides a large number of "safe" days both before and after ovulation.

4. *Sympto-thermal method.* Use of changes of temperature, cervical mucus, and the cervix itself during fertile periods make this an extremely effective method. Probably demands the least abstinence while providing the greatest protection.

Please be aware that the above descriptions are in no way designed to teach you all you need to know about a method to use it effectively. If you decide to pursue any of them, you should purchase a concise book on the subject, learn the method well, and then *follow the rules.* Failures in these methods are usually attributed to "cheating"!

Sometimes couples wonder if abstinence is harmful to the marriage relationship. From all the evidence, it appears not to be. Most couples who practice natural family planning find that there are other, equally effective ways of expressing love at this time, and that the brief separation makes their "reunion" that much sweeter and more honeymoon-like.

If you enjoyed a "natural" birth, are now practicing "natural" breastfeeding, and have a desire to avoid any chemicals or devices that are "unnatural" or abortive, maybe natural family planning is just what you've been looking for!

METHODS OF CONTRACEPTION

METHOD	"THE PILL"	"MINI-PILLS"	INTRAUTERINE DEVICE (IUD)*	DIAPHRAGM WITH SPERMICIDAL JELLY OR CREAM
WHAT IS IT?	Pills with two hormones, an estrogen and progestin, similar to the hormones a woman makes in her own ovaries.	Pills with just one type of hormone: a progestin, similar to a hormone a woman makes in her own ovaries.	A small piece of plastic with nylon threads attached. Some have copper wire wrapped around them. One IUD gives off a hormone, progesterone.	A shallow rubber cup used with a sperm-killing jelly or cream.
HOW DOES IT WORK?	Prevents egg's release from woman's ovaries, makes cervical mucus thicker and changes lining of the uterus.	It may prevent egg's release from woman's ovaries, makes cervical mucus thicker and changes lining of uterus, making it harder for a fertilized egg to start growing there.	The IUD is inserted into the uterus. It is not known exactly how the IUD prevents pregnancy.	Fits inside the vagina. The rubber cup forms a barrier between the uterus and the sperm. The jelly or cream kills the sperm.
HOW RELIABLE OR EFFECTIVE IS IT?	99.7% if used consistently, but much less effective if used carelessly.	97-99% if used perfectly, but less effective if used carelessly.	97-99% if patient checks for string regularly.	About 97% effective if used correctly, but much less effective if used carelessly.

*Publisher's Note: The IUD is effective because it prevents a *fertilized egg* from implanting itself in the uterine wall. Technically, this is an induced *abortion*. Therefore we strongly recommend that the IUD not be used.

HOW WOULD I USE IT?	Either of two ways: 1. A pill a day for 3 weeks, stop for one week, then start a new pack. 2. A pill every single day with no stopping between packs.	Take one pill every single day as long as you want to avoid pregnancy.	Check string at least once a month right after the period ends to make sure your IUD is still properly in place.	Insert the diaphragm and jelly (or cream) before intercourse. Can be inserted up to 6 hours before intercourse. Must stay in at least 6 hours after intercourse.
ARE THERE PROBLEMS WITH IT?	Must be prescribed by a doctor. All women should have a medical exam before taking the pill, and some women should not take it.	Must be prescribed by a doctor. All women should have a medical exam first.	Must be inserted by a doctor after a pelvic examination. Cannot be used by all women. Sometimes the uterus "pushes" it out.	Must be fitted by a doctor after a pelvic exam. Some women find it difficult to insert, inconvenient, or messy.
WHAT ARE THE SIDE EFFECTS OR COMPLICATIONS?	Nausea, weight gain, headaches, missed periods, darkened skin on the face or depression may occur. More serious and more rare problems are blood clots in the legs, the lungs, or the brain, and heart attacks.	Irregular periods, missed periods, and spotting may occur and are more common problems with mini-pills than with the regular birth control pills.	May cause cramps, bleeding, or spotting; infections of the uterus or of the oviducts (tubes) may be serious. See a doctor for pain, bleeding, fever, or a bad discharge.	Some women find that the jelly or cream irritates the vagina. Try changing brands if this happens.
WHAT ARE THE ADVANTAGES?	Convenient, extremely effective, does not interfere with sex, and may diminish menstrual cramps.	Convenient, effective, does not interfere with sex, and less serious side effects than with regular birth control pills.	Effective, always there when needed, but usually not felt by either partner.	Effective and safe.

U.S. DHEW Publication No. (HSA) 76-16000

Second section of chart, METHODS OF CONTRACEPTION

METHOD	SPERMICIDAL FOAM, JELLY OR CREAM	CONDOM ("RUBBER")	CONDOM AND FOAM USED TOGETHER	PERIODIC ABSTINENCE (NATURAL FAMILY PLANNING)	STERILIZATION
WHAT IS IT?	Cream and jelly come in tubes; foam comes in aerosol cans or individual applicators and is placed into the vagina.	A sheath of rubber shaped to fit snugly over the erect penis.		Ways of finding out days each month when you are most likely to get pregnant. Intercourse is avoided at that time.	Vasectomy (male). Tubal ligation (female). Ducts carrying sperm or the egg are tied and cut surgically.
HOW DOES IT WORK?	Foam, jelly and cream contain a chemical that kills sperm and acts as a physical barrier between sperm and the uterus.	Prevents sperm from getting inside a woman's vagina during intercourse.	Prevents sperm from getting inside the uterus by killing sperm and by preventing sperm from getting out into the vagina.	Techniques include maintaining chart of basal body temperature, checking vaginal secretions, and keeping calendar of menstrual periods, all of which can help predict when you are most likely to release an egg.	Closing of tubes in male prevents sperm from reaching egg; closing tubes in female prevents egg from reaching sperm.

HOW RELIABLE OR EFFECTIVE IS IT?	About 90-97% effective if used correctly and consistently, but much less effective if used carelessly.	About 97% effective if used correctly and consistently, but much less effective if used carelessly.	Close to 100% effective if both foam and condoms are used with every act of intercourse.	Certain methods are about 90-97% if used consistently. Other methods are less effective. Combining techniques increases effectiveness.	Almost 100% effective and NOT usually reversible.
HOW WOULD I USE IT?	Put foam, jelly or cream into your vagina each time you have intercourse, not more than 30 minutes beforehand. No douching for at least 8 hours after intercourse.	The condom should be placed on the erect penis before the penis ever comes into contact with the vagina. After ejaculation, the penis should be removed from the vagina immediately.	Foam must be inserted within 30 minutes before intercourse and condom must be placed onto erect penis prior to contact with vagina.	Careful records must be maintained of several factors: basal body temperature, vaginal secretions and onset of menstrual bleeding. Careful study of these methods will dictate when intercourse should be avoided.	After the decision to have no more children has been well thought through, a brief surgical procedure is performed on the man or the woman.
ARE THERE PROBLEMS WITH IT?	Must be inserted just before intercourse. Some find it inconvenient or messy.	Objectionable to some men and women. Interrupts intercourse. May be messy. Condom may break.	Requires more effort than some couples like. May be messy or inconvenient. Interrupts intercourse.	Difficult to use method if menstrual cycle is irregular. Sexual intercourse must be avoided for a significant part of each cycle.	Surgical operation has some risk but serious complications are rare. Sterilizations should not be done unless no more children are desired.

WHAT ARE THE SIDE EFFECTS OR COMPLICATIONS?	Some women find that the foam, cream or jelly irritates the vagina. May irritate the man's penis. Try changing brands if this happens.	Rarely, individuals are allergic to rubber. If this is a problem, condoms called "skins" which are not made out of rubber are available.	No serious complications.	No complications.	All surgical operations have some risk but serious complications are uncommon. Some pain may last for several days. Rarely, the wrong structure is tied off or the tube grows back together. There is no loss of sexual desire or ability in vast majority of patients.
WHAT ARE THE ADVANTAGES?	Effective, safe, a good lubricant and can be purchased at a drugstore.	Effective, safe, can be purchased at a drugstore; excellent protection against sexually transmitted infections.	Extremely effective, safe, and both methods may be purchased at a drugstore without a doctor's prescription. Excellent protection against sexually transmitted infections.	Safe, effective if followed carefully; little if any religious objection to method. Teaches women about their menstrual cycles.	The most effective method; low rate of complications; many feel that removing fear of pregnancy improves sexual relations.

U.S. DHEW Publication No. (HSA) 76-16030.

WORKING TOGETHER

Daily Practice Session

Below is a "mock labor" to practice every day until the birth of your baby. Role play different situations that could occur in the course of labor (to better prepare you for any and everything). Be sure to vary your position. During these rehearsals, the coach should practice all of his coaching techniques and adapt them to the personal needs of the mother. Using suggested time intervals, this practice should take approximately one hour.

Progress	*Contractions*
Early Labor: Dilatation: 1/-4 cm. Contractions: 5 min. apart	1 60-sec. contraction—slow deep chest 1 60-sec. contraction—accelerate from slow deep chest to fast deep chest, 15-sec. peak. 1 60-sec. contraction—accelerate from fast deep chest to slow pant, 15-sec. peak.
Half-way: Dilatation: 5-6 cm. Contractions: 4 min. apart.	1 60-sec. contraction—accelerate from fast deep chest to slow pant, 20-sec. peak. 1 75-sec. contraction—accelerate slow pant to med. pant, 20-sec. peak.
Active Labor: Dilatation: 7-8 cm. Contractions: 3 min. apart	2 75-sec. contractions—accelerate slow pant to fast pant, 20-sec. peak. 2 75-sec. contractions—accelerate med. pant to fast pant, 30-sec. peak. 2 90-sec. contractions—accelerate med. pant to fast pant, two 15-sec. peaks.
Transition: Dilatation: 8-10 cm. Contractions: 2½ min. apart	1 90-sec. contraction—accelerate med. pant to pant-blow, three 15-sec. peaks

	2 2-min. contractions—pant-blow to blow, three 15-sec. peaks.
Birth:	1 60-sec. contraction—pushing.
Contractions: 4 min. apart	2 60-sec. contractions—crowning.
Placenta	1 pushing contraction—one push, 10 sec.

Continue neuromuscular exercises, possibly between contractions. Continue all other exercises.

Topics for Discussion and Action
1. *Coach*: In what areas do you think your wife will need more help and understanding during the postpartum period?
2. Discuss specific plans for the postpartum recovery period.
3. *Wife*: What areas of responsibility do you think will be especially hard to maintain immediately after giving birth? (that is, having dinner ready on time, teaching a Sunday school class, caring for other children).
4. What plans and preparations can be made *now* to make the above items less burdensome?

PART III

HOW TO "GROW" A CHILD

Teach us what we shall do unto the child that shall be born.
(Judg. 13:8)

Introduction to Part III

We mentioned in the first part of this book that a child is similar to a tender young plant, needing certain conditions in order to develop properly. We discussed the "soil" which has to be prepared—a stable family life and a good relationship between the parents. Your childbirth classes may have done much to help you understand each other during the critical times of pregnancy, postpartum, and new parenthood, but your *real* strength will come from a living faith in God, the Designer of families.

Imagine a garden, filled with an assortment of flowers in many varieties and a rainbow of colors—soft pink, deep red, sparkling yellow, pale blue, and spring green. The blend of fragrances is almost intoxicating. Though they are collectively beautiful, it becomes quickly apparent that no two flowers are identical; while all the seeds may have been sown at the same time, the resulting plants vary in their size and maturity. At the outset, the gardener had no idea which seed would produce the largest, prettiest flower. But he did know how to maximize the potential of each one, by providing them with the necessary elements: sunlight, water, fertilizer, and protection from insects.

Your baby is, in many ways, a seedling. Although every child is different, each is the beginning of a creative masterpiece by God, to be tended and nurtured, loved and enjoyed, by you, the "gardeners." Parenting practices vary greatly from one family to another, but successful and satisfied parents know that certain things must be provided in order for our offspring to mature in all aspects of life.

The chapters which follow comprise a "gardening guide," offering scriptural insights and suggestions for parents new to the business of "child-growing."

CHAPTER 10

Sunlight

Truly the light is sweet, and a pleasant thing it is for the eyes to behold the sun. (Eccles. 11:7)

Since all plants need a certain amount of light each day, we might call the first basic need of children "sunlight"—an all-encompassing warmth that surrounds the child from earliest infancy, assuring him of the beauty of the world he has entered and telling him of God's care. Children learn love by example, and they learn trust and confidence by having their needs met. Our Heavenly Father meets *our* needs, usually before we even ask: "Before they call, I will answer; and while they are yet speaking, I will hear" (Isa. 65:24). "The Lord is nigh unto them that call upon him" (Ps. 145:18).

Can we do less for our own children? The needs of an infant are simple: food, warmth, and physical contact. These are needs that were met automatically when the baby lived inside his mother. His mother and father are logically the ones to meet those needs on the outside. Because of the bond of attachment God designed parents and babies to form, no one can satisfy a baby better than his parents.

Feeding a baby when he first expresses hunger is one of the best ways to first show God's love to your child. It helps him to know that the world is all right, that there is someone "out there" who cares how he feels, and upon whom he can depend. This will aid him in later years as he learns to trust God, as well as other people. "Thou didst make me trust when upon my mother's breasts" (Ps. 22:9, NASB).

Another way to help your baby feel the "sunlight" of God's love is with lots of caressing and cuddling. In the "real world" the things we avoid touching are those which are *repulsive* to us—prickly plants and slimy creatures—not warm, lovable people! Yet, some parents are afraid that too much physical contact will "spoil" a child. This is not so. If your baby is held when he desires to be held, he can't help but get the message, "I am loved!" Don't be surprised if, resultantly, he desires even more close contact with you. This is his way of saying "I love you, too!"

The amount of "sunlight"—closeness and security—your child needs will be fairly consistent throughout the first two years of his life. But the ways in which you will provide this will vary. At first, the major concern will be to meet his physical needs and the need for a stable and calm environment. Within just a few weeks after birth, however, most babies are ready for more action; and since children *learn* through *play*, the hours you spend having fun with your child is time most profitably spent.

During the winter months, plants appear to get along on far less sunlight. There will be times, as your child grows older, when he will increasingly entertain himself, play with friends, read, or pursue other interests. He will seem to need less and less of your "sunlight." Always remember that the need is present, even if it doesn't show itself at particular times in his life. He learns about God's continuous love and concern through his parents' continuous love and concern.

A MESSAGE FOR FATHERS*

by Dr. Lee Salk

These days, the joys and rewards of fatherhood are too often ignored.

The man who gives his children tenderness, as well as strength, gets back more than a full measure of happiness, while his children gain the emotional support they need.

Fathers have unfortunately been pressured into a rather narrow role as parents. As a father myself, and as a psychologist who

---

*Riverside, CA *Press-Enterprise*, June 17, 1973. Reprinted by permission.

has a very special interest in children and parents, I feel that fatherhood is the achievement of one of the most marvelous experiences in life: the creation of another human being.

It represents an unparalleled challenge to nurture a new life, protect it, help it grow and develop, and watch proudly as it becomes more independent.

Fatherhood is clearly an important role, particularly with regard to the mental health of children. Research has shown that boys whose fathers were gone during their first years of life had more behavioral difficulties later on than boys whose fathers were present. These children seem to have had more trouble establishing relationships with both adults and children.

Other studies show that a clear relationship exists between anti-social behavior in boys and the absence of a strong male figure to identify with during childhood. A strong figure is one who is not only consistent, but also one who is protective and loving.

Studies have also shown that a young boy's degree of masculine interest depends to a great deal on the image he has of his father. The more masculine boys tend to see their fathers as more powerful as well as more nurturant—that is to say, loving and giving.

This idea tends to demolish the concept that if you want a "manly son" you must be tough and aggressive. On the contrary, you must be manly and also be tender.

CHAPTER 11

Water

I will pour water upon him that is thirsty . . . and my bless-ing upon thine offspring. (Isa. 44:3)

The self-image a child develops will largely determine his happiness in life. If he likes himself and accepts his abilities, he can adjust to whatever life dishes out to him. According to Dr. Bruce Narramore, "if he develops a negative self-image, he may struggle through life with feelings of depression, anxiety, guilt or anger."[1] We as parents need to help our children develop proper self-esteem.

When a baby is born he has no self-concept. He develops a sense of who he is through the reactions of others to him—how he is treated. He quickly measures his worth by the responsiveness ("sunlight") of his parents. If he is given attention, caressed, smiled at, sung to, and played with, the foundations are laid for the baby to acquire a healthy self-esteem.

As the baby gets older, parental "sunlight" alone can no long-er adequately fulfill the child's needs. Just as a plant cannot live long on sunlight alone, but needs water to sustain life, so your baby begins to need "water"—esteem-building words of praise—to insure that he does not "wilt."

Do not let any unwholesome talk come out of your mouths, but only what is helpful for building others up according to their needs, that it may benefit those who listen. (Eph. 4:29, NIV)

When you spend time showing genuine interest in your child, speaking words of kindness, and encouraging his progress, the message comes across to him loud and clear: "I am special." We all like to know that we are important to someone. Children *thirst* to know this. When we praise a child, it is important that it be for specific deeds rather than as a value judgment on his personality. "You are such a good boy" is not nearly as effective as "You are a real help to me when we go shopping."

There is another side to this coin—what we say can *tear down* a child's feeling of worth.

Death and life are in the power of the tongue. (Prov. 18:21)

Bruce Narramore says, "Every criticism is a blow to the child's self-image. Each compliment helps to build an inner sense of confidence."[2] Many parents have the erroneous idea that it is their duty to point out all their child's faults. They think they are helping; instead, they are forcing the child to think that he can't do anything right.

Dishonest praise can do just as much harm to a child's self-esteem as can criticism. Children are very sensitive to our true feelings. They know when we do not really mean what we say. They learn to distrust us so that even honest praise has no effect. They begin to "wilt" from lack of "water." A toddler or preschooler may express this in misbehavior. This matter should always be considered if we notice sudden changes or negative behavior in our young children. Following is a checklist for "watering" your child's self-image. Periodically, throughout each day, ask yourself: "In what ways can I build up my child today?"

HOW IS A HEALTHY SELF-CONCEPT BUILT INTO A CHILD?*

	YES	NO
1. With the parent's voice.		
Do I speak my child's name with pleasure?	_____	_____
Do I use my child's real name rather than a nickname?	_____	_____
Do I use words like "stupid, naughty, messy, selfish, etc.," on my children?	_____	_____

*Used by permission of Life Action Ministries, Buchanan, Michigan.

Do I frequently yell at my child when I ____ ____
want him to do something?

Do I talk about my child in positive ways ____ ____
when he is listening?

2. With the parent's facial expression.

   Do I communicate to my child with eye ____ ____
   contact?

   Do I communicate to my child through ____ ____
   my facial expression?

3. Through proper non-verbal communication.

   Do I cause my child to *feel* loved by me? ____ ____

   Do I make my child think I consider his ____ ____
   work juvenile or childish?

4. Through avoiding comparison.

   Do I compare my child with other ____ ____
   children?

   Do I feel self-conscious about something ____ ____
   unchangeable in my child?

   Do I use my child to satisfy my own ____ ____
   unfulfilled ambitions?

5. By being lavish in praise and appreciation.

   Do I praise my child for positive inner ____ ____
   qualities or actions I appreciate?

   Do I make only positive comments about ____ ____
   my child when he is listening?

6. By training to assume responsibility.

   Do I fail in my example of responsibility ____ ____
   by making promises to my child and
   forgetting to keep them?

Does my child have assigned
responsibilities within the home? _____ _____

Do I make sure he follows through with _____ _____
his responsibilities?

7. By putting courtesy first.

Do I treat my child with courtesy? _____ _____

Do I express an interest in things my _____ _____
child wants to share with me?

Remember, you represent Jesus Christ's leadership and authority to your child. He will formulate his confidence in God and himself from your success in instilling a healthy concept of worth in him.

How Do I Begin?

1. Establish in your child's mind that a change in operation is taking place.
2. Express gratitude that he is your child.
3. Acknowledge your failure in not accepting your child as God's unique design.
4. Ask his forgiveness.
5. Begin immediately to apply the above guidelines.

CHAPTER 12

Food

Whatsoever things are true, whatsoever things are honest, whatsoever things are just, whatsoever things are pure, whatsoever things are lovely, whatsoever things are of good report; if there be any virtue, and if there be any praise, think on these things. (Phil. 4:8)

No one would deny that sunlight and water are the two primary needs of every growing plant. If these are met, one's garden will usually survive. But most gardeners agree that to have a successful garden of superior appearance and fruit requires fertilizer and/or compost to enrich the soil and nourish the plants. And it will not suffice for the gardener to peel back the petals of a rosebud and dump plant food inside the flower. The nourishment has to penetrate the soil, enter the plant's roots, and work its way to the very heart of the organism, allowing the flower to bloom *from the inside out.*

There is a wonderful parallel between this process and the "growing" of a child. Plant food can be compared to the attitudes, ideals, and reinforcement that the child receives in his day-to-day experience at home—the positive or negative mental attitudes and impressions he encounters in his parents. And the blooming process is the gentle and gradual unfolding of that child's personality, encouraged and aided by the "food" of his environment.

The discussion of temperaments by Dr. Tim and Beverly LaHaye provides some of the most interesting and easily applied "psychology" we have encountered. According to the LaHayes, there are four major personality divisions. Most of us have one predominant temperament combined with one other of lesser degree. Each temperament has its own characteristic strengths and weaknesses. A person with a "good personality" is one who has learned, with God's guidance, to overcome his weaknesses and maximize his strengths to their fullest potential. This should be our goal for our children. Here is a brief look at the four temperaments:

Sanguine. Perhaps the most easily-recognized of all the temperaments, the sanguine person is happy, vivacious, enthusiastic, warm and friendly. On the weakness side, he is disorganized, often lacking in discipline, easily swayed, and rather undependable. The sanguine person has many good ideas and loads of enthusiasm, but he has difficulty actually getting things accomplished.

Choleric. A choleric individual is self-disciplined, optimistic, confident, determined, a real "go-getter" and achiever. Unfortunately, he also has tendencies toward anger, impatience, coldness, bitterness, and short temper.

Melancholic. The melancholic person is generally more introverted and reserved than either of the preceding two. This person is creative, sensitive to others, analytical, practical, artistic, dependable, meticulous and self-sacrificing. His weaknesses are excessive worry and doubt, a critical spirit, pessimism, self-centeredness, pride and moodiness.

Phlegmatic. This is perhaps the "coolest" of all temperaments. This person is usually quiet and reserved, easy-going, and enjoyable to be with. He is careful and practical, almost overly cautious. On the negative side, this person is slow, unmotivated, teasing, and stubborn. He has a tendency to make fun of the weaknesses found in other temperaments.

Obviously, no one's personality consists of just one temperament. Many of us are a combination of two and in every individual you can observe a unique balance of strengths and weaknesses. A person who has his weaknesses under control and who is utilizing his strengths will be a "nice person" regardless of his temperament. God made you the way you are, totally different from any other person, because He has a special plan for a person with your combination of attributes.

As for your child, a unique, inborn, and God-given temperament can begin to reveal itself at a very early age. You can exert tremendous influence on many of your child's ideas, preferences, and attitudes, but you cannot change his underlying temperament. No gardener would plant corn and then expect to harvest tomatoes, yet a parent may do essentially the same thing by insisting that his child strive to be something incompatible with his temperament. You cannot expect a shy child to become aggressive, or a spontaneous, impulsive child to become reticent and thoughtful, any more than you can expect a cornstalk to bear tomatoes.

You can, and should, look for your child's strong points and emphasize them. You can also work with him on minimizing his weaknesses. But you *have* to give him freedom to be whatever it is God wants him to be.

When you begin "peeling off petals"—force-feeding him— you destroy the individual beauty of the child, and his true potential may be forever lost.

How are you "feeding" your little growing child? With the negative food of critical words, harsh tones and looks of displeasure? Or with the positive nutrients found in warm acceptance, praise for accomplishments, frequent kind words, and a positive outlook on life?

Many have read, at some time, the following lines by Dorothy Law Nolte; but it takes real commitment by parents to heed the lesson of these words:*

> If a child lives with criticism, he learns to condemn.
> If a child lives with hostility, he learns to fight.
> If a child lives with ridicule, he learns to be shy.
> If a child lives with shame, he learns to feel guilty.
> If a child lives with tolerance, he learns to be patient.
> If a child lives with encouragement, he learns confidence.
> If a child lives with praise, he learns to appreciate.
> If a child lives with fairness, he learns justice.
> If a child lives with security, he learns to have faith.
> If a child lives with approval, he learns to like himself.
> If a child lives with acceptance and friendship, he learns to find love in the world.
>
> Dorothy Law Nolte

*Used by permission.

Just as plant food joins with sunlight and water to enhance the health and beauty already present in a plant, the positive acceptance you "feed" your child will work with the watering of self-esteem and the sunlight of agape love to create a beautiful masterpiece, delightfully unique, a tribute to its Creator.

CHAPTER 13

Protection from Insects

And the rain descended, and the floods came, and the winds blew, and beat upon that house; and it fell not: for it was founded upon a rock. (Matt. 7:25)

What gardener hasn't faced the problem of insect invasion? This can be a frustrating experience, especially for an amateur! He entertains visions of lush plants and flowers, and abundant fruits and vegetables, without a mar or scratch. What a disappointment to one day find the entire melon patch consumed by snails, or the roses overtaken by aphids!

Our greatest enemies in the business of child-growing are the forces of Satan in their various disguises. They would love to devour our "crops," and they will try to get an early start. We must begin even *earlier* than they if we want to protect our children from "insects."

The world in which we live has many philosophies and attitudes which contradict those God established in Scripture. Those values are presented to us daily in newspaper and magazine articles, and television programs. Now children are being raised *permissively* (without limits), *humanistically* (in the belief that the child is innately good and his wrongdoings are a result of parental mistakes and a repressive environment), and *impersonally* (by surrogate mothers and baby-sitters). Immorality and lawlessness are becoming commonplace in our society; a child who has not received adequate training and guidance from his parents will be most vulnerable to the influence of such ungodly trends. Sending him to Sunday school once a week is not enough—God established families long before He established the church. He intended that parents teach their children.

Strong and healthy plants are more resistant to insect attacks than those which are weak to begin with. It is imperative that you strengthen your child spiritually. Then he can resist the "insects" of modern thought. It is a long battle, and a seemingly endless one, but here are some things that may help you in the spiritual training of your child:

1. Make sure your own life is a good example. The most powerful sermon your child will ever receive is the one acted out in his parents' lives.

2. Pray *for* him and *with* him daily. In this way he will come to know that "the Lord is nigh unto all them that call upon him" (Ps. 145:18).

3. Put your prayers into action by arming your children with principles from God's Word: "These commandments that I give you today are to be upon your hearts. Impress them on your children. Talk about them when you sit at home and when you walk along the road, when you lie down and when you get up" (Deut. 6:6, 7, NIV).

Ideally the teaching of biblical principles should be a part of the family's daily living. Children less than a year old will clap and bounce to the rhythm of lively, happy "Sunday school" songs and choruses. And many two-year-olds will try with all their might to sing along. Children of two are also capable of memorizing and reciting short verses and truths, which, if reinforced, will remain with them the rest of their lives. The learning must be enjoyable and kept at the child's level of development, but it can take place at any time of day. We can sing with our children, tell stories of Jesus, and talk of God's love while driving in the car, doing housework, bathing them—any time at all!

You should also establish a daily family time of learning (even once a week is better than none at all, but make sure the program is *consistent* and *enjoyable*). Many feel that a daily period of family worship cannot begin too soon in a child's life. The wise gardener takes measures to *prevent* insects *before* they destroy his crops. You may never know how early your child begins to absorb what you're saying and retain it in his heart. If the daily devotions become a habit, it will always be easier to discuss spiritual truths with your child, because you will be providing the opportunity for such discussion. And when the child indicates readiness for spiritual decisions such as accepting Christ as Savior, you will not miss the chance, since you will be "tuned in" to his spiritual needs just as you are to his physical, mental, and emotional needs.

The family devotional time should be geared to the age and maturity of the children involved. The average backyard gardener does not hire a planeload of pesticide bombs to solve the insect problem in his six-square-yard plot. In the same way, family devotions should be short and, above all, a pleasant experience for the child. With a baby or toddler it is sufficient to sing a couple of songs like "Jesus Loves Me" or the "B-I-B-L-E," talk about God's love or His Son Jesus for a moment, and then pray briefly. Then the child can be allowed to play or sit quietly nearby while Mommy and Daddy have a short time of study, prayer, or whatever they feel is warranted. It is important to remain flexible. If your child is overtired or hungry, the family time may be better put off for a while, so that it remains enjoyable to all. We cannot expect small children to have the endurance of adults!

As the baby becomes a toddler and begins to understand more, short Bible stories can be included. Just be sure they don't become complicated, boring, or otherwise disinteresting to little ears. The small child's time should last only five to eight minutes, as that is about the maximum span you will hold his interest. Of course, any child who wishes to sing or pray more, or hear more stories should be encouraged. Watch your child for clues. You'll be amazed at his interests and abilities, even at an early age. Babies of eight months or so may clap their hands while the others sing—what a delightful way for them to express that they are having a good time!

Dr. James Dobson, noted Christian psychologist and author, has compiled a "Checklist for Spiritual Training" which is included on the following pages. Use it to measure your child's progress as he grows and requires more complex training. Also many excellent books are available to help you begin a family devotional time with your children. These are listed in the book list, and are available at your Christian bookstore or from the publishers.

A CHECKLIST FOR SPIRITUAL TRAINING*

by Dr. James Dobson

I was recently asked why some children grow up to reject God, even though they have been raised in Christian homes and exposed to church services and religious instruction. Some adults display no appreciation or understanding of the values their parents thought they had taught them. To their utter dismay, Mom and Dad learn too late that their training just didn't "take."

Each time I see this occur, I am reminded of the story of Eli in the Old Testament. The devoted priest failed to save his own boys, both of whom became profane and evil young men. What disturbs me most, however, is that the saintly Samuel—one of the greatest men in the Bible—witnessed Eli's parental mistakes, yet proceeded to lose his children, too!

The message is loud and clear to me: God will not necessarily save our children as a reward for our own devotion! Christianity is not inherited by the next generation. We must do our early homework if we are to be successful in this vital responsibility.

Parents have been commanded to "train up a child in the way he should go." But this poses a critical question: What way *should* he go? If the first seven years represent the "prime time" for religious training, what should be taught during this period? What experiences should be included? What values should be emphasized?

It is my strong belief that a child should be exposed to a carefully conceived, systematic program of religious training. Yet we are much too haphazard about this matter. Perhaps we would hit the mark more often if we clearly recognized the precise target.

Following is a checklist for parents—a set of targets at which to aim. Many of the items require maturity which children lack, and we should not try to make adult Christians out of immature youngsters. But we can gently urge them toward these goals—

---

*Used by permission.

these targets—during the impressionable years of childhood.

Essentially, the six scriptural concepts which follow should be consciously taught, providing the foundation on which all future doctrine and faith will rest. I encourage every Christian parent to evaluate his child's understanding of these six areas:

CONCEPT I—"And thou shalt love the Lord thy God with all thy heart" (Mark 12:30).

1. Is your child learning the love of God through the love, tenderness, and mercy of his parents? (most important)
2. Is he learning to talk about the Lord, and to include Him in his thoughts and plans?
3. Is he learning to turn to Jesus for help whenever he is frightened or anxious or lonely?
4. Is he learning to read the Bible?
5. Is he learning to pray?
6. Is he learning the meaning of faith and trust?
7. Is he learning the joy of the Christian way of life?
8. Is he learning the beauty of Jesus' birth and death?

CONCEPT II—"Thou shalt love thy neighbor as thyself" (Mark 12:31).

1. Is he learning to understand and empathize with the feelings of others?
2. Is he learning not to be selfish and demanding?
3. Is he learning to share?
4. Is he learning not to gossip and criticize others?
5. Is he learning to accept himself?

CONCEPT III—"Teach me to do thy will; for thou art my God" (Ps. 143:10).

1. Is he learning to obey his parents as preparation for later obedience to God? (most important)
2. Is he learning to behave properly in church—God's house?
3. Is he learning a healthy appreciation for both aspects of God's nature: love and justice?

4. Is he learning that there are many forms of benevolent authority outside himself to which he must submit?
5. Is he learning the meaning of sin and its inevitable consequences?

CONCEPT IV—"Fear God, and keep his commandments: for this is the whole duty of man" (Eccles. 12:13).

1. Is he learning to be truthful and honest?
2. Is he learning to keep the Sabbath day holy?
3. Is he learning the relative insignificance of materialism?
4. Is he learning the meaning of the Christian family, and the faithfulness to it which God intends?
5. Is he learning to follow the dictates of his own conscience?

CONCEPT V—"But the fruit of the Spirit is . . . self-control" (Gal. 5:22-23, RSV).

1. Is he learning to give a portion of his allowance (and other money) to God?
2. Is he learning to control his impulses?
3. Is he learning to work and carry responsibility?
4. Is he learning to tolerate minor frustration?
5. Is he learning to memorize and quote scripture?

CONCEPT VI—" . . . he that humbleth himself shall be exalted" (Luke 14:11).

1. Is he learning a sense of appreciation?
2. Is he learning to thank God for the good things in his life?
3. Is he learning to forgive and forget?
4. Is he learning the vast difference between self-worth and egotistical pride?
5. Is he learning to bow in reverence before the God of the universe?

In summary, your child's first seven years should prepare him to say, at the age of accountability, "Here am I, Lord. Send me!"

CHAPTER 14

Pruning

Train up a child in the way he should go: and when he is old he will not depart from it. (Prov. 22:6)

What book for new parents is complete without a section on discipline? Most parents, whether new or experienced, are concerned about how to apply God's instructions to "train" their children.

We compare the discipline process to that of pruning a tree, because, just as pruning helps to shape the tree into something more attractive, the function of discipline is similar:

Correct thy son and he shall give thee rest; yea, he shall give delight unto thy soul. (Prov. 29:17)

Many couples, in their early zeal not to raise a "spoiled brat," have a limited picture of discipline; to them it includes only one thing: spanking or other punishment for undesirable behavior—and this at a surprisingly early age.

A dictionary definition states that discipline is much more: "Instruction, training that corrects, molds, or perfects." In fact, the word "train" as used in Proverbs relating to our children, comes from the Hebrew *chânak*, which means "to dedicate, give instruction." Viewed in its proper perspective, there are many aspects to discipline; they are not incompatible with one another, but work together to form a complete system.

Kids Will Be Kids

When I was a child, I spake as a child, I understood as a child, I thought as a child; but when I became a man, I put away childish things. (1 Cor. 13:11)

The various levels of childhood produce various types of behavior. We parents need to understand this; we must know the stages of child development and be able to apply that knowledge in the training of our own children. Children are *not* miniature adults. They cannot be expected to possess adult emotions, judgment, wisdom, or stamina before their time. How many of us, even in our twenties and thirties, act "childishly" on occasion? Yet many parents are exasperated when their three-year-old *acts* like a three-year-old. It is important to relate to a child at his own level, to see the world through his eyes, and to feel the emotions he feels. How is this done?

As we mentioned earlier, formation of a parental bond at birth is a major factor in the relationship you have with your child, even years later. Parents who are actively involved in the birth process and who are allowed to "bond" shortly afterward have much less difficulty understanding their child's needs and behavior.

It is also helpful to have, for your own reference, a well-written book on child development. You will then be able to analyze your baby's or child's actions in light of what is "normal" for that age. And you will usually find him to be remarkably typical!

For Crying Out Loud!

Weep with them that weep. . . . (Rom. 12:15)

Crying is a form of communication. Before a child can talk, his methods of expressing his thoughts, feelings, needs, and desires are limited to "body language" (facial expressions, gestures), vocalizations, and crying. And the younger the baby, the more limited he is.

A tiny newborn doesn't know how to request a meal politely. He has no knowledge of etiquette, and probably doesn't even know that it is food he wants. He can't tell time to see if he's "supposed" to be hungry yet. All he knows is that the gnawing in his tummy is somewhat painful, somewhat frightening, and *very* real.

But how do you deal with crying? When a baby cries, there is a reason. Ask yourself a few questions: Is he tired, hungry, or frustrated about something? Does he need pacifying? (Babies need to suck a lot, not only when feeding.) Is he bored or scared?

Has his routine been disrupted by company or travel? Does he have a painful or itchy rash? Is he hot? Is he thirsty? Does he need a walk outdoors? Does he need to be held and cuddled, rocked and nursed?

The old assumption that babies should be left to "cry it out" if they have been fed, changed, and do not have a pin sticking them is rather weak, as far as the needs of a baby go.

Maybe it would help to put things into perspective if you asked yourselves, "What would Jesus do if He had been an earthly parent?"

Is your baby hungry? Scripture commands us to feed even our enemies if they are hungry. Can we do any less for those dearest to our hearts?

Is he scared? Our Lord said, "Fear not, for *I am with you.*"

Is the baby waking at night? Jesus invites us to "come unto me . . . and I will give you rest."

What is he crying about? Jesus promised that those who mourn will be comforted.

Many parents are concerned about what seem to be "tantrums" in the small baby. While we agree that there is nothing more unbecoming than uncontrolled anger in an older child, with an infant it is pitiful because in most cases it can be prevented.

Mothers will tell you that these displays of "anger" occur, for the most part, on two occasions: (1) when the mother leaves the baby; and (2) when, by her failure to respond to his *initial* request for food (or rest, or loving attention, or any other reasonable need), she makes him *think* she has abandoned him.

Anger is often found to be present with the emotion of grief. It is a common psychological response, and defense, to become angry when we lose someone we love. Generally, the unexplained disappearance of one's mother is enough to produce severe grief, especially if that person is an infant who's not at all certain that Mommy will be back! Although it is not desirable, anyone can become angry if he is repeatedly or continuously thwarted and denied basic needs such as food, sleep, or security. The Bible acknowledges that it is possible to provoke anger (wrath) in a child, but at the same time warns parents *not* to do it (Eph. 6:4).

You can help your baby avoid much unnecessary anger by responding to his needs appropriately, as he expresses them.

Sometimes this may mean feeding or holding your child even though it is not convenient for you. Or maybe it will mean not leaving him with a sitter for a while if separation is too hard on him. Separation from mother can be a very painful thing for young children. Even if she is just in another room, if the baby does not sense she is nearby, she might as well be on another planet. Just because someone has told you your baby "needs" to learn to get along without you doesn't make it so—*our Lord never instructed us to get along without Him.* In fact, He encourages reliance upon our loving heavenly Father. And He promised He would always be available to us: "Lo, I am with you always" (Matt. 28:20). "I will never leave thee, nor forsake thee" (Heb. 13:5).

As your child matures, he will be able to be separated from you. He will also learn about anger and how to deal with it after you teach him. But a person must be able to understand what is expected of him before he can learn what is right to do.

Crying is as normal to a baby as asking questions is to a three-year-old. If crying and other normal infant behaviors are not considered as cause for "punishment" during the first months of a child's life, the question of discipline is largely answered. For more information on avoiding problems *before* they begin, keep reading!

Creepy Crawlers

As your baby grows and begins to get around on his own, you will find that he has an enormous curiosity and a desire to learn about things. He will try to investigate and explore everything within reach. At the same time, he becomes much more capable of expressing his wishes and preferences, and his love for you. These newly acquired abilities mean your baby will probably do things you sometimes wish he wouldn't. But if you recognize his tendencies and his interests, you can take two positive steps in "discipline" to make it both easy and fun for baby to do what's right: prevention and distraction.

A nine-month-old we know (very well!) is a classic example of this "exploring" stage. Left alone in the bathroom for two minutes while his mother answered the phone, he managed to empty the wastebasket, dump out the diaper pail, unwind half a roll of toilet paper into the toilet, and then go "fishing." His mother was faced with several options:

1. She could get mad (not advisable).
2. She could ignore him (not safe).
3. She could *distract* him with another activity, expressing her distress as she removes him from the bathroom and closes the door behind her.
4. She could have *prevented* it in the first place by taking him with her when she left the room. (We live and learn!)

The latter two are basic and effective tools in the area of positive discipline.

Prevention

Let . . . no man put a stumbling block or occasion to fall in his brother's way. (Rom. 14:13)

Prevention *must* be exercised in every home that has small children. It is the only way a mother with a busy creeper or an active toddler can have any peace of mind. Get down on the floor for a child's-eye view. What do you see? Fascinating tables filled with knick-knacks, wall sockets with the most interesting little holes, brightly colored books and magazines, tasty-looking houseplants, a lamp perfect for climbing! What would *you* do if you had never experimented with those items before, had been gazing curiously at them for months, and had suddenly gained mobility?

Remove the "breakables," store poisons up high, cap your electrical outlets, and close the toilet lid (better yet, close the whole bathroom door!). Even wastebaskets may have to be hidden in closets for a while, but why tempt him with things that are going to cause conflict? An added benefit of a "babyproof" home is that when your friends bring *their* babies over, you can still relax and have a good time. For even if you are successful at keeping your own child out of everything (which is not conducive to preserving your sanity!), it will be much harder to do the same with someone else's baby. If you detest the "bare look" for your house, invest in some noninjurious wood or plastic goodies to spruce up your decor.

Another aspect of prevention is that of eliminating the circumstances that produce annoying behavior. Does your baby scream when he gets overtired or overstimulated? Then how about a relaxing walk or warm bath before bedtime to help him unwind? Or try listening to some soft, pretty music with the lights lowered.

Does he shriek and bang on his highchair tray every second you are not feeding him? Then load up his tray with "finger food" and let him feed himself.

Does he cry whenever you walk out of the room? This is normal behavior beginning at 6 to 8 months. He is discovering that he LOVES you, and wants to be with the one he loves. Whenever possible, take him with you and avoid the tears.

Someday he will learn that Mommy and Daddy always return and that he can trust them to meet his needs fully. Until that day comes, *show him*.

Distraction

God is faithful, who . . . will with the temptation also make a way to escape. (1 Cor. 10:13)

Despite our well-intentioned measures, we know that not all conflicts can be prevented. Babies are far too imaginative for that! Undoubtedly your baby will discover the one thing in your house that you thought he couldn't disturb, and will set out to prove you wrong! Or he'll concentrate the one type of behavior that you cannot stand and haven't yet figured out how to prevent.

At this time, we put into effect tool number two: distraction. A low shelf of books, an older child's toys that have small pieces, or a variety of colorful items are among the intriguing objects that necessitate distraction. It's really very simple: hand him an object that he *can* play with and move him to a different area. The combination of those two actions will, in many cases, cause him to lose interest in whatever it was he was getting into. Depending on the temperament of your child, you may or may not have to repeat this several times to get the message across.

Distraction is also successful if the child is cranky, whining, or otherwise unhappy. It can tide you over while you are checking out of the grocery store or waiting in the doctor's office (try peeka-boo, pat-a-cake, or "this little piggy"). A fussy baby can usually be distracted by being taken outdoors—weather permitting, or for a walk through the house. While you're changing his diaper, a squirmy infant can be handed a toy to interest him.

Always remember that there is an underlying cause for his behavior, and do your best to find out that cause as soon as possible.

You will notice that our "pruning tools" for the first year, or so, have been positive in nature. There is a reason for that—we feel that a baby's initiation in this world should be positive. The early part of a child's life should be a happy time as he learns that "life on the outside" isn't bad. At birth a baby doesn't know if he has been pushed into the hands of friend or foe—he must have *proof* that life is good.

Of course there will be times when you have to say "no," and take appropriate action for his own good, but these times don't have to be nearly as frequent as most people think. Some people believe that the reason one of baby's first words is usually "no" is because that's all he has been hearing for months before!

Learning the meaning of "no" is an important function from about 9 months on. Dr. James Dobson says that at about 15 months is the time when a child actually begins to test parental limits to see if they really mean what they say (he's hoping that they do!). When this takes place, it is important that parents react confidently and decisively, and show him lovingly but firmly that he must obey for his own health and welfare.

Dr. Dobson's books on child-rearing, especially *The Strong-Willed Child*, give excellent insight as to how to accomplish this without creating feelings of resentment or frustration in either the child or parent.

The key to all discipline (training, teaching, motivating) is LOVE. Discipline without love is merely punishment, and serves no purpose but to create resentment and distrust. A child will accept almost any boundaries if he knows they are placed in genuine love and concern for his well-being. This type of training, teaching, and motivating will not only heighten your child's self-esteem, but it will also promote peace and harmony, happiness, and love in the home, and create a truly joyful family beginning.

Glossary of Terms

ACTIVE PHASE—The period of labor in which dilatation from 4-8 cm. takes place. This is usually when a woman has to really start *working* with her contractions.

AMNIOTIC FLUID—Waterlike fluid surrounding the baby *in utero*. Acts as a shock absorber for the baby, prevents heat loss, and equalizes pressure on the baby.

AMNIOTIC SAC—Membranous bag lining the uterus. Also known as the "bag of waters" because it contains the amniotic fluid.

ANALGESICS—Drugs which relieve pain without necessarily inducing sleep.

ANESTHETICS—Drugs which completely block pain impulses, resulting in a loss of feeling or sensation.

APGAR SCORE—A method of rating the newborn's condition at birth. Two points are possible in each of five different categories: appearance (color), pulse (heartbeat), grimace (response to stimuli), activity (muscle tone), and respiration (breathing). A total of ten points is possible, two points for each category. Anything over 6 is considered good, but most unmedicated babies have scores of 8-10. The score is determined at one minute after birth and again at five minutes.

AREOLA—The dark-colored skin surrounding the nipple of the breast.

BIRTH CANAL—Another name for the vagina, or the passageway through which the baby travels to be born.

BREECH—A positioning of the baby in the uterus in which the buttocks or feet instead of the head are presenting at the cervix.

CENTIMETERS—A metric measurement used to describe dilatation. Most women need to dilate about 10 centimeters before the baby can pass through the cervical opening. Some people measure dilatation in "fingers" (one finger = two centimeters).

CERVIX—The narrow, muscular neck of the uterus which opens into the vagina.

COLOSTRUM—The "first milk" available to the baby. Produced by the breasts during pregnancy and in the days before the actual milk comes in. It is high in protein content, contains immunity factors, and acts as a mild laxative to clear the intestine of the first bowel movements, or meconium.

CONDITIONING—The process of learning to respond in a certain manner to a certain stimulus.

DILATATION (or *dilation*)—The gradual opening of the cervix to permit passage of the baby. This occurs during the contractions of first-stage labor.

EFFACEMENT—The thinning and shortening of the cervix, which usually occurs before dilatation takes place. In some women, particularly those who have had a baby before, it may occur simultaneously with the early part of dilatation.

EFFLEURAGE—A light, circular massage of the abdomen during labor. May be done by the woman or her coach, and is used to help maintain release of the abdominal muscles and at the same time provide another point of concentration for the laboring mother.

ENEMA—The introduction of a solution (or plain water) into the rectum and colon to empty the lower intestine. This is sometimes a routine part of admission to the hospital. By having the colon empty, more room is provided for the baby to pass, and there is better maintenance of cleanliness during delivery.

EPISIOTOMY—An incision made in the perineum to enlarge the birth opening.

FETAL MONITOR—An electronic device which can detect and record the baby's heart tones *in utero*, and also the frequency and intensity of the mother's contractions.

HYPERTONIC CONTRACTIONS—Strong contractions that produce little or no progress.

HYPOTONIC CONTRACTIONS—Weak, ineffective contractions that do not produce normal labor progress.

INDUCTION AGENT—Hormones given either intravenously,

intramuscularly, or in the form of tablets or nasal spray to cause labor to begin or to help the progress of a slow-moving labor.

JAUNDICE—A condition occurring in some newborns as their bodies attempt to break down and dispose of extra red blood cells acquired at birth. Bilirubin is produced and manifests itself as a yellowish tinge to the skin. Most causes of jaundice are physiologic, or normal, occurring between three and seven days of age, and disappear by themselves. If you have doubts, consult your doctor.

KEGEL EXERCISES—Tightening and releasing the muscles which comprise the "pelvic floor" and serve to support all of the internal structures of the body (pubococcygeus muscles).

LATENT PHASE—The earliest stage of dilatation during labor, when the cervix is effacing and dilating 0-4 centimeters.

LET-DOWN REFLEX—The process by which the breasts eject milk upon stimulation of the baby's sucking. Relaxation and confidence are the best ways to assure a good let-down reflex. Sometimes just thinking of the baby or hearing one cry will trigger the let-down reflex in a mother.

MULTIPARA—A woman who has had one or more previous births.

NEUROMUSCULAR—Controlling the actions of certain muscles by signals from the brain.

PERINEUM—External tissues surrounding the anus and external genitals.

PLACENTA—The organ developed during pregnancy through which nutrients and oxygen are transferred to the baby and carbon dioxide is transferred back to the mother. At term, it is about the size of a dinner plate, weighs about 1½ pounds, and looks like a piece of raw liver. Also known as the "afterbirth."

POSTERIOR—A presentation of the baby in which the back of the baby's head lies nearer the mother's spine, thus causing a longer labor, and if the baby remains posterior for the second stage, more pushing is required.

POSTPARTUM—The period of time following the birth when the mother recuperates and the baby begins to become integrated into the family. It is a time of recovery and readjustment for the whole family, and things should be kept as calm as possible.

PRECIPITATE LABOR—An extremely fast-moving labor.

"PREP"—The procedure followed when a woman enters the hospital for delivery. May include an enema and a partial shave of pubic hair.

PRIMIPARA—A woman who is pregnant for the first time.

PROLONGED LATENT PHASE—Defined by the first part of dilatation (0-4 cm.) lasting longer than 20 hours in the primipara and 13½ hours in the multipara.

ROOMING-IN—The policy in some hospitals of allowing mother and baby to share the same room for all or most of the day, and sometimes at night, too. Rooming-in allows the two to become acquainted sooner and with more ease, and is beneficial to breastfeeding because the frequent sucking occurring when "feeding on demand" causes the mother's milk to come in sooner.

SILVER NITRATE—A substance placed in the baby's eyes at birth to prevent infection should the mother have gonorrhea. In some states it is permissible to use an alternate treatment that is milder and less irritating to the eyes. If not, the silver nitrate can be washed out with sterile water after it has done its job. Remember, babies don't have tears to rinse their own eyes!

THRESHOLD OF SENSATION—The level of intensity a stimulus must reach in a particular person before it is admitted to the brain for interpretation. One of the goals of your training is to raise your threshold of sensation.

TOXEMIA—A toxic condition of late pregnancy, often thought to be due to faulty nutrition. Symptoms include headache, blurred vision, albumin in the urine, edema, sudden weight gain, increased blood pressure. If caught early enough, symptoms may be eliminated by eating 125 grams of protein a day. Toxemia is not usually found in women whose protein intake was 80-100 grams a day to begin with. However, the exact cause is not known and the only cure is the delivery of the placenta.

TRANQUILIZERS—Drugs which relieve anxiety and promote calmness without inducing sleep or lessening pain.

TRANSITION—The end of the first stage of labor, dilatation 8-10 centimeters. Most difficult time for women to cope with, but also the shortest period of labor.

UMBILICAL CORD—The "lifeline" between mother and baby. Connects baby's umbilicus (navel) to the placenta—the baby's source of food and oxygen. Cord can be anywhere from several inches to three feet long; average is about 20 inches.

UTERUS—Muscular organ which contains the baby. In the non-pregnant woman it is pear-like in size and shape. During pregnancy it expands to accommodate the baby, the placenta, and the amniotic fluid.

VAGINA—The curved, very elastic canal, 5-6 inches long, which connects the cervix to the eternal genital area. Also known as the "birth canal."

VERNIX CASEOSA—A white, cheeselike substance found on the baby's skin at birth. It has served as a protective coating *in utero*. It can be rubbed into the skin to prolong its effects.

Suggestions for Additional Information

A wise man will hear and will increase learning; and a man of understanding shall attain unto wise counsels. (Prov. 1:5)

Our thoughts expressed in this book have been gleaned, to a great extent, from other sources, not the least of which is God's Word. Our intent has been to compose these ideas in such a way that new light will be shed upon one of the oldest subjects around: becoming parents.

We are indebted to those authors and authorities who provided ideas for us in their works listed below. We recommend that you read as much as you can from the following sources. The ones marked with an asterisk (*) are *highly* recommended as a basic library for all expectant parents.

MARRIAGE ENRICHMENT

Andelin, Helen. *Fascinating Womanhood.* New York: Bantam, 1975. Ideas for women to add excitement and real love to a marriage.

Brandt, Henry, Ph.D., and Phil Landrum. *I Want My Marriage to Be Better.* Grand Rapids: Zondervan, 1976. Easy, light reading with practical suggestions for both partners.

Christenson, Larry and Nordis. *The Christian Couple.* Minneapolis: Bethany Fellowship, 1975. Insights on the meaning of love, authority and submission in marriage.

Deutsch, Ronald. *The Key to Feminine Response in Marriage.* New York: Random House, 1968. Importance of the pubococcygeus (Kegel) muscles and exercises for their strengthening and toning.

*Dobson, James, Ph.D. *What Wives Wish Their Husbands Knew About Women.* Wheaton: Tyndale House, 1976. An interesting analysis of what things are *really* important to women, and what a man can do to help.

Kippley, John and Sheila. *The Art of Natural Family Planning.* Cincinatti: Couple to Couple League, 1977. The book that most thoroughly describes all aspects of female fertility cycles and how to avoid or achieve pregnancy by proper "timing."

*LaHaye, Beverly. *The Spirit-Controlled Woman.* Irvine, CA: Harvest House, 1976. How a woman can use the work of the Holy Spirit in her life to enhance her own temperament.

*LaHaye, Tim, Ph.D., and Beverly. *The Act of Marriage.* Grand Rapids: Zondervan Co., 1976. A detailed look at the beauty of sexual love in marriage from a Christian standpoint.

LaHaye, Tim, Ph.D. *How to Be Happy Though Married.* Wheaton: Tyndale House, 1973. Suggestions for easing the adjustments that accompany every marriage.

LaHaye, Tim, Ph.D. *Understanding the Male Temperament.* Old Tappan, NJ: Revell, 1977. Clarifies the characteristics of temperament as they apply to adult males. Helps wives to better relate to their husbands.

Sproul, R. C. *Discovering the Intimate Marriage.* Minneapolis: Bethany Fellowship, 1975. Guidelines for developing an intimate marriage on every level, on the assumption that the right kind of intimacy is the key to a happy marriage.

Trobisch, Ingrid. *The Joy of Being a Woman: What a Man Can Do.* New York: Harper & Row, 1975. An easy-to-read explanation of the cycles and changes in women and how these affect her physical, emotional, and spiritual feelings and needs.

*Wheat, Ed, M.D., and Gaye. *Intended for Pleasure.* Old Tappan, NJ: Fleming H. Revell Co., 1977. A book encompassing all aspects of sex in the Christian marriage, including a section on sex during pregnancy.

Wheat, Ed, M.D. *Love Life.* Grand Rapids, Mich.: Zondervan Publishing House, 1980. Taken from Dr. Wheat's popular seminar, this book conveys methods of restoring love and excitement to an "ordinary" marriage.

PREGNANCY AND BIRTH

Bean, Constance A. *Labor and Delivery: An Observer's Diary.* Garden City, NY: Doubleday, Inc., 1977. Real observations of several labors and deliveries, ranging from highly medicated to totally "natural."

Bing, Elisabeth, RPT. *The Adventure of Birth.* New York: Simon & Schuster, 1970. Personal accounts of the use of Lamaze techniques.

Bing, Elisabeth, RPT. *Six Practical Lessons for an Easier Childbirth.* New York: Grosset and Dunlap, 1967. Six abbreviated Lamaze classes.

Bradley, Robert A., M.D. *Husband Coached Childbirth.* New York: Harper & Row, 1965. A good discussion of the father's importance in pregnancy and childbirth, but very negative regarding Lamaze preparation.

Chabon, Irwin, M.D. *Awake and Aware.* New York: Dell, Inc., 1969. This book helps break down the negative attitudes toward childbirth and presents the case for prepared childbirth.

Dick-Read, Grantly, M.D. *Childbirth Without Fear.* New York: Harper and Row, 1949. The new fourth edition, revised and edited by Helen Wessel and Harlan Ellis, M.D., is more readable, concise, and practical than previous editions.

Donovan, Bonnie. *The Caesarean Birth Experience.* New York: Random House, 1977. Practical, comprehensive, and reassuring guide to family-centered caesarean birth.

*Elkins, Valmai Howe. *The Rights of the Pregnant Parent.* New York: Two Continents, 1976. Helps couples make informed choices regarding alternatives in childbirth.

Ewy, Rodger and Donna. *Preparation for Childbirth.* New York: Pruett, 1970. A basic manual of Lamaze technique as applied in the average labor and delivery. Some prenatal exercises are also included.

Hanes, Mari. *The Child Within.* Wheaton: Tyndale House, 1979. A devotion and Bible study booklet covering the nine months of pregnancy for expectant mothers.

*Hazell, Lester Dessez. *Commonsense Childbirth.* New York: G. P. Putnam's Sons, 1969. A concise guide dealing with all aspects of preparation for birth: nutrition, prenatal care, childbirth classes, emergency childbirth, postpartum care. A MUST!

Jacobson, Edmund, M.D. *How to Relax and Have Your Baby.* New York: McGraw Hill, 1965. A classic by one of the pioneers in the study of relaxation as related to childbirth.

Karmel, Marjorie. *Thank You, Dr. Lamaze.* Garden City, N.Y.: Dolphin Books, 1965. A personal account, by the woman who brought the Lamaze method to the United States, of what the training meant to her in the births of her two children.

Kitzinger, Sheila. *The Experience of Childbirth.* New York: Penguin Books, 1978. Deals with the emotional factors of pregnancy and birth as well as the physical. Contains exercises and techniques for a more comfortable birth using the "psychosexual" method. Excellent for building confidence and removing fears.

Klaus, Marshall H., M.D., and Kennell, John H., M.D. *Maternal-Infant Bonding.* St. Louis: C. V. Mosby Co., 1976. Explains the authors' earlier "imprinting" theory of bonding. Still informative.

Lamaze, Fernand. *Painless Childbirth.* New York: Pocket Books, 1970. A practical, detailed course in psychoprophylactic techniques.

Leboyer, Frederick. *Birth Without Violence.* New York: Knopf, Inc., 1975. Sensitively written account of what the baby *may be* experiencing during birth and what can be done about it.

Macaulay, Susan Schaeffer. *Something Beautiful From God.* Westchester, Ill.: Cornerstone Books, 1980. Strikingly illustrated with color photographs, this book will help you and your children better understand the miracles of conception, pregnancy, and childbirth.

Mendelsohn, Robert S., M.D. *Confessions of a Medical Heretic.* New York, N.Y.: Warner Books, 1979. An intriguing look at some of the practices of modern medicine and why they should be used with discretion. Very enlightening reading.

Montagu, Ashley. *Life Before Birth.* New York: New American Library, 1977. Details development of the baby from the moment of conception and offers ideas for optimum health and development.

Nilsson, Lennart. *A Child Is Born*. New York: Dell, Inc., 1965. Beautiful color photographs and descriptions of fetal development.

*Parfitt, Rebecca Rowe. *The Birth Primer*. Philadelphia: Running Press, 1977. Examines all the options available to expectant parents, including place of birth, medical care, and types of preparation. *Very* complete!

Randall, Cher. *Total Preparation for Childbirth*. Plainfield, NJ: Logos, Int., 1977. Written by a Christian Lamaze instructor, this book offers spiritual preparation as well as physical and emotional. Also a large section on home births.

Vellay, Pierre. *Childbirth Without Pain*. New York: E. P. Dutton & Co., 1960. Dr. Lamaze's associate-in-practice writes a detailed series of classes in the Lamaze method. Very scientific and "deep" reading, but it clarifies the whole method well.

*Wessel, Helen. *The Joy of Natural Childbirth*. New York: Harper and Row, 1976. Originally published under other titles, this work is a detailed examination of scripture that outlines God's plan for women giving birth.

*White, Gregory J., M.D. *Emergency Childbirth*. Franklin Park, IL: Police Training Foundation, 1977. Good for all prospective fathers to read, "just in case."

Wright, Erna. *The New Childbirth*. New York: Simon & Schuster, 1971. Covers reproduction, nutrition, labor and delivery, and parenting in a delightful British manner.

NUTRITION

*Brewer, Gail-Sforza & Tom, M.D. *What Every Pregnant Woman Should Know*. New York: Penguin Books, 1979. Discussion of the importance of a balanced, nutritious diet during pregnancy and how good nutrition can prevent many of the physical maladies commonly occurring in pregnancy. Also contains many recipes.

Coffin, Lewis A., M.D. *The Grandmother Conspiracy Exposed*. Santa Barbara, CA: Capra Press, 1974. An interesting and often amusing exposé of the facts and fallacies concerning your child's nutrition.

Goldbeck, Nikki & David. *The Supermarket Handbook*. New York: Signet, 1976. How to find nutritious, whole foods on your grocery shelves.

Helmer, Barbara Sloan. *The Better Baby Food Cookbook*. Minneapolis: Bethany Fellowship, 1980. Preparation, storage and serving of mother-made baby foods which "grow" with the infant.

Kenda, Margaret Elizabeth, and Phyllis Williams, R.N. *The Natural Baby Food Cookbook*. New York: Avon, 1972. Lots of good ideas for the introduction of solid food to baby's diet.

Lansky, Vicki. *Feed Me, I'm Yours*. Wayzata, MN: Meadowbrook Press, 1974. How to make good eating habits exciting and fun for children.

Lansky, Vicki. *The Taming of the C.A.N.D.Y. Monster*. Wayzata, MN: Meadowbrook Press, 1974. Creative and interesting snacks to replace "junk food" for little (*or* big) people.

Lappe, Francis Moore. *Diet for a Small Planet*. New York: Ballantine, 1971. Ways to get more protein for your money by combining certain "incomplete" proteins to form complete ones.

Larson, Gena. *Better Food for Better Babies*. New Canaan, Conn.: Keats Publishers, 1972. Recipes and ideas for babies' first foods. Also many allergy recipes.

*Smith, Lendon, M.D. *Feed Your Kids Right*. New York, N.Y.: McGraw-Hill, Inc., 1979. Examines the important role children's diet plays in determining how they act. Details how much negative behavior can be eliminated with nutritional changes. Extremely worthwhile!

Williams, Phyllis, R.N. *Nourishing Your Unborn Child*. New York: Avon Books, 1975. Basic prenatal nutrition information with a selection of recipes.

BREASTFEEDING

(Mothers planning to nurse should have for easy reference at least one of the books marked with an asterisk below.)

Brewster, Dorothy Patricia. *You Can Breastfeed Your Baby . . . Even in Special Situations*. Emmaus, PA: Rodale Press, 1980. The perfect book to encourage women who often don't breastfeed because of handicaps, extensive hospitalization, multiple births, prematurity, allergies, etc. Extensive.

*Eiger, Marvin S., M.D., and Sally Wendkos Olds. *The Complete Book of Breastfeeding*. New York: Bantam, 1972. A very detailed guide, answering most questions parents are likely to have.

Kippley, Sheila. *Breastfeeding and Natural Child Spacing*. New York: Penguin Books, 1974. Outlines clearly to what extent breastfeeding acts to decrease fertility. A warm book on "natural mothering."

*La Leche League, International. *The Womanly Art of Breastfeeding*. Franklin Park, IL: La Leche League, 1978. An easily readable collection of all the ideas and information necessary for successful breastfeeding, written cheerfully and optimistically.

*Pryor, Karen. *Nursing Your Baby*. New York: Harper and Row, 1963. An excellent book, dealing with all the necessary "how-tos" plus much on the emotional bond between mother and baby.

Raphael, Dana. *The Tender Gift: Breastfeeding*. New York: Schocken Books, 1973. Stresses the necessity of "mothering the mother" to create an atmosphere conducive to successful breastfeeding.

CHILD-REARING AND FAMILY LIVING

(Entries marked *CD are books on Child Development, from which you should select at least one. Those marked *FD are books which will be helpful to you in establishing a family devotional time. Books with only an asterisk [*] are generally related to other areas of child-rearing, discipline, and family harmony.)

Alexander, Olive J. *Developing Spiritually Sensitive Children*. Minneapolis: Bethany Fellowship, Inc., 1980. Bible basis and practical applications for creating an atmosphere where children can develop spiritual sensitivity.

Allison, K. J. *Teaching Children as the Spirit Leads*. Plainfield, NJ: Logos International, 1977. Great ideas for taking advantage of a child's interests and using them to teach spiritual truths.

Brandt, Henry, Ph.D., and Phil Landrum. *I Want to Enjoy My Children.* Grand Rapids: Zondervan, 1975. Easy to read. Many suggestions for the peaceful management of children in the home.

*CD Brazelton, T. Berry, M.D. *Infants and Mothers: Differences in Development.* New York: Dell, 1969. Follows the development of three babies, slow, average, and active, through each month of their first year.

*Campbell, D. Ross, M.D. *How to Really Love Your Child.* Wheaton: Victor Books, 1977. Stresses the *expression* of the love that we know is there but often doesn't show.

*Christenson, Larry. *The Christian Family.* Minneapolis: Bethany Fellowship, 1970. A million-seller on family-living. Contains two basic sections: "God's Order for the Family" and "Practicing the Presence of Jesus."

*FD Coleman, William. *The Good Night Book.* Minneapolis, MN: Bethany Fellowship, 1979. Simple devotions for preschool-aged children on topics of concern to them, such as darkness, sharing, and dreaming.

*FD Coleman, William. *Today I Feel Like a Warm Fuzzy.* Minneapolis, MN: Bethany Fellowship, 1980. Devotions covering the wide range of emotions experienced by children. Will help your child accept himself and learn to cope with the feelings he has.

Cook, Barbara. *How to Raise Good Kids.* Minneapolis, MN: Bethany Fellowship, 1978. The author is convinced that "the Bible requirements of a mother are refreshingly simple."

Dobson, James, Ph.D. *Dare to Discipline.* Wheaton: Tyndale House, 1970. Helpful insight on discipline for parents trying to decide what procedures to follow.

Dobson, James, Ph.D. *Hide or Seek.* Old Tappan, NJ: Revell, 1974. A look at the child's self-esteem: what it is and how to build it and help shape it.

*Dobson, James, Ph.D. *The Strong-Willed Child.* Wheaton: Tyndale House, 1978. Sets forth the Judeo-Christian philosophy of child-rearing and compares it with contemporary ideas. Excellent!

Dobson, James, Ph.D. *Straight Talk to Men and Their Wives.* Waco, Texas: Word Books, 1980. A candid look at the author's insight on men's roles—methods of relating to your wife, children, employer, friends, and God.

*Jacobsen, Margaret Baily. *What Happens When Children Grow*. Wheaton: Scripture Press, 1977. Step-by-step development of the child physically, emotionally, mentally, and spiritually, from birth to pre-adolescence. Highly recommended.

*FD Jahsmann, Allan Hart and Martin P. Simon. *Little Visits With God*. St. Louis: Concordia, 1957. Short stories emphasizing spiritual truths for families with children ages 4-10.

*CD LaHaye, Beverly. *How to Develop Your Child's Temperament*. Irvine, CA: Harvest House, 1977. Follows the child's development from birth through the teen years and helps parents to deal specifically with each child's individual temperament.

*LaHaye, Tim and Beverly. *Spirit-Controlled Family Living*. Old Tappan, NJ: Revell, 1978. A guide for a harmonious home life.

Meier, Paul D., M.D. *Christian Child Rearing and Personality Development*. Grand Rapids: Baker Book House, 1977. Dealing with the emotional struggles of growing up, from a Christian viewpoint.

Merrell, JoAnn. *Tree of Life*. Minneapolis: Bethany Fellowship, 1980. A devotional book for families with small children. Includes poster-size tree to which children attach "leaves."

Narramore, Bruce, Ph.D. *Help! I'm a Parent!* Grand Rapids: Zondervan, 1977. Creative alternatives to constant corporal punishment in discipline.

*Narramore, Bruce, Ph.D. *Parenting with Love and Limits*. Grand Rapids, Mich.: Zondervan Publishing House, 1979. A scriptural look at the role of parenthood and all that God designed it to be. An excellent book for studying together—workbook also available.

*CD Newton, Niles, M.D. *The Family Book of Child Care*. New York: Harper and Row, 1957. Explores all the various ages and stages of childhood and answers almost every question about child care and child-rearing imaginable.

The Open Home. New York: St. Martin's Press, Inc., 1976. Beautifully illustrated with hundreds of color photographs, this is a collection of ideas for making your home the best learning environment your child can have. Many tips on dealing with children.

*Poland, Donna. *Handle With Care*. Arrowhead Springs, CA: Campus Crusade for Christ, Int., 1976. A 40-hour workbook-course to improve mother-child relationships. Excellent for mothers of *any* age child.

*FD Taylor, Kenneth. *The Bible in Pictures for Little Eyes*. Chicago: Moody Press, 1979. Short, accurate Bible stories accompanied by beautiful illustrations. Appropriate for even the youngest listeners.

Thevenin, Tine. *The Family Bed*. Minneapolis, MN: (Distributed by La Leche League, Franklin Park, IL.) 1976. Offers support and encouragement for parents of youngsters with sleeping problems.

HOME BIRTH

Brooks, Tonya, and Linda Bennett. *Giving Birth at Home*. Cerritos, CA: Association for Childbirth at Home International, 1976.

Hazell, Lester Dessez. *Commonsense Childbirth*. New York: G. P. Putnam's Sons, 1969.

Sousa, Marion. *Childbirth at Home*. New York: Bantam Books, 1977.

Ward, Charlotte and Fred. *The Home Birth Book*. Washington, D.C.: Inscape Corporation, 1976.

Additional Resources

Association for Childbirth at Home
P.O. Box 1219
Cerritos, CA 90701

Dads Only
An interesting little monthly newspaper with lots of ideas for
creative fathering—games, topics for discussion, book reviews,
crafts, all in a Christian framework. Subscription is $11.50 per
year from P.O. Box 340, Julian, CA 92036.

Focus on the Family
(Source of books, pamphlets, tapes, and radio and TV broadcast
information by Dr. James Dobson)
P.O. Box 500
Arcadia, CA 91006

Home Oriented Maternity Experience
511 New York Avenue
Tacoma Park, Washington, D.C. 20012

La Leche League International
(Printed literature on every aspect of breastfeeding, and information on groups near you.)
9616 Minneapolis Ave.
Franklin Park, IL 60131

Ed Wheat, M.D.
(Author of cassette albums *Love-Life* and *Sex Technique and
Sex Problems in Marriage*.) They may be ordered from him at:
130 Spring St.
Springdale, AR 72764

Birth Report Form

We would like to hear from you after your baby's birth! If you wish to report your birth experience to us, please include the following:

Father's name and age

Mother's name and age

Address

Father's occupation

Mother's occupation

Previous births—how many, and what preparation used, if any

Information about the classes you attended—name of teacher, name of sponsor, cost, number of classes in series, and, if they were not Genesia classes, what techniques were taught that differ from the ones described in this book.

Place of birth

Doctor

Information about baby—name, weight, length, Apgar score

Date and time of birth

Details of labor and delivery—Be sure to include how you recognized the onset of labor, what the contractions felt like, when you notified the doctor, whether or not the labor was "normal," any difficulties you encountered, any medications or procedures administered, how you recognized transition, and anything you would do differently next time. Also, please include your personal thoughts and feelings regarding your labor and birth.

Mail to: Genesia Childbirth Educators, 706 N. Cambria, Anaheim, CA 92801.

And be sure to make an extra copy to keep in your baby book!

Genesia Childbirth Educators

BOARD OF CONSULTANTS

Kenneth Akey, M.D.
Orange, Ca.

Thomas Bellino, Ph.D.
Alexandria, Va.

James Dobson, Ph.D.
Los Angeles, Ca.

Edwin Ford, M.D.
Newport Beach, Ca.

Sandy Gardner
Yorba Linda, Ca.

Gilly Kuehn
Anaheim, Ca.

Beverly LaHaye
El Cajon, Ca.

Tim LaHaye, Ph.D.
El Cajon, Ca.

Beverlee McClung, R.N.
Newport Beach, Ca.

Rev. Bruce Smith
Centralia, Missouri

Pierre Vellay, M.D.
Paris, France

Helen Wessel
La Mesa, Ca.

Ed Wheat, M.D.
Springdale, Ark.

Gaye Wheat
Springdale, Ark.

Genesia Childbirth Educators is a group of born-again Christian Lamaze instructors dedicated to promoting better family beginnings among parents, Christian and non-Christian alike. "Genesia" (je-ne-SEE-a) is the Greek word for "birthday." We offer complete preparation for couples anticipating their child's *very* first birthday.

If you have questions or problems related to your pregnancy, birth, or postpartum, or if you'd like information about classes in your area, we are glad to help. Just write to our headquarters: Genesia, 706 N. Cambria, Anaheim, CA 92801.

We want to help you discover God's plan for you during these wonderful "beginning" years.

He . . . shall gently lead those that are with young. (Isa. 40:11)

CHRISTIAN CHILDBIRTH EDUCATORS' REGISTRY

We hope Genesia will eventually expand to every part of the United States and even some foreign countries. However, since all our officers and instructors must put the Lord and their families as their first priorities in life, our growth will not be as rapid as that of some organizations. To "fill the gap" in the areas where Genesia classes are not yet being conducted, we are compiling a registry of Christian Childbirth Educators throughout the world.

If you are a born-again believer currently teaching childbirth preparation classes, we would like to add your name to our files. Please include:

    Name
    Address
    Phone number and area code
    Method taught
    Affiliation with any organization
    Number of classes in series
    Please include also a brief synopsis of your course
       (i.e., what topics are covered in each class).

Notes

PART I

Chapter 1

1. Ellen Roweton and Singcord Recordings, 1976. Used by permission.

2. Dr. Ed Wheat, "Love-Life" Seminar, Long Beach, Ca., Grace Brethren Church, September 14-15, 1979.

Chapter 2

1. Ibid.

2. Helen Wessel, *The Joy of Natural Childbirth* (New York: Harper & Row, 1978).

3. Klaus, Marshall, "The Biology of Parent-to-Infant Attachment," *Birth and the Family Journal* (Winter, 1978), Vol. 5:4, pp. 200-203.

PART II

Chapter 3

1. Longacre, Doris Janzen, *More-With-Less Cookbook* (Scottdale, PA: Herald Press, 1976), pp. 34-35. Used by permission.

2. Hazell, Lester Dessez, *Commonsense Childbirth* (New York: G. P. Putnam's Sons, 1969), p. 143.

Chapter 4

1. Janet Moss, "Editorial," *Pep Talk* (October, 1976: Kansas City, Mo.). Used by permission.

2. Rosemary Cogan, "The Unkindest Cut?", *Contemporary Ob/Gyn* (Vol. 9, April, 1977).

3. Rebecca Rowe Parfitt, *The Birth Primer* (Philadelphia, PA: Running Press, 1977), pp. 86-90. Adapted by permission of Running Press.

Chapter 5

1. Ibid., p. 6. Reprinted by permission of Running Press.

Chapter 6

1. Graph reprinted by permission of Corometrics, Inc., Wallingford, Conn.

Chapter 7

1. Avis J. Ericson, *Medications Used During Labor and Birth* (Milwaukee, Wis.: International Childbirth Education Association, 1977). Adapted into chart form by permission of ICEA.

Chapter 8

1. Niles Newton, *The Family Book of Child Care* (New York: Harper & Row, 1957), pp. 391, 392. Used by permission.

2. Used by permission of California Department of Health.

Chapter 9

1. Ruth Hulburt Hamilton, "Song for a Fifth Child," first appearing in *Ladies Home Journal*, October, 1958.

2. Helen Andelin, *Fascinating Womanhood* (Santa Barbara, CA: Pacific Press, 1963). Adapted by permission.

3. Adapted by permission of Bethany Medical Center, Kansas City, KS.

PART III

Chapter 11

1. Bruce Narramore, *Help! I'm a Parent!* (Grand Rapids: Zondervan Publishing House, 1972), p. 113.

2. Ibid., p. 123.